Suze Fair

ALL THE LIES I'VE LOVED BEFORE

Discover the joy
that comes
with an Honest
& Authentic life.

Cover art and interior hand-lettering: Jordan Kurzen
Layout: Andy Kurzen
Author photo: Zach Zino
Editors: Amelia Graves and Jenn Amatuzzo

For Kelly Fair

Who would I be without all these years of TOGETHER?
You have taught me what it means to love and be loved BIG.
With my whole heart.

For Ben, Katie, and Mackenzie

Being your mother has taught me what it means to belong.
No matter how you got to me, you are mine and I am yours.
For now and forever more.

CONTENTS

Forward

by Nancy Beach

The invitation struck me as a little odd. Don't most people celebrate big birthdays when launching a new decade? We've all been to parties for someone turning 30, 40, 50, etc. But this one, for my friend Suze, was to mark her 45th birthday. And it would be no small little party, but an entire weekend in the Bahamas with Suze and 7 girlfriends from various parts of her life. A donor couple supplied the magnificent home where we gathered to honor our friend. Over the course of the long weekend, the number 45 began to make sense. Suze experienced the alarm of a cancer diagnosis at ages 15, 25, and 35. While she did endure some other major health challenges in her mid 40's, the "C" word was not a concern at 45. And that was cause for great relief and joy.

Over that glorious weekend (complete with a chef who created our outstanding meals!), I treasured the opportunity to see Suze with other women who like me, consider her to be a "best friend." In moments of raucous laughter and tender vulnerability, we shared our many memories of how Suze showed up for us and how deeply we delight in her.

For about 30 years now, I have had the privilege of calling Suze my friend. We first met as young moms and women in ministry who took a seat at tables with mostly, if not all, men. We began to learn one another's stories. A few times each year, we meet halfway between our home cities at a Bob Evans restaurant in Valparaiso, Indiana. That journey of two hours each way is more than worth it as we reconnect over too many Diet Cokes, eager to hear all about one another's families, faith journey, ministry challenges, and health updates. We listen with love, nodding our heads, and frequently saying, "Yes, me too." There may also be some venting, seeing one another as a safe place to poke into what has been hurtful and hard. We always tip the Bob Evans waitress generously after sitting in the booth for long stretches while other people come and go. My introverted husband cannot imagine how Suze and I find so much to talk about that a few hours is never quite enough.

When I think of Suze, two primary words leap out—fierce and intentional. Suze has experienced more pain and challenge than most of us. She is a fighter. I am frequently inspired by the resilience Suze displays as she faces yet another challenge or comes up against one more barrier. So much of what Suze and all of us battle are the voices in our heads that feed us lies and seek to defeat us. In this book, Suze boldly identifies those deadly lies and explores how to kick them out and replace them with truth.

Along with being fierce, Suze is intentional. I see this intentionality vividly in Suze's approach to faith, marriage, motherhood, friendship, and work. Suze is the opposite of passive. She moves toward the pain, the learnings, the conflict. Noone asks me more probing questions than Suze. Sometimes it's a bit annoying! But I know her heart is full of love and a desire to see me flourish. That longing for others to grow fueled the writing of these pages. Suze's journey has purpose because she leverages the learnings and invites us to join her on a courageous journey.

I encourage you to read this book somewhat slowly. Examine the voices in your own head, the lies that linger and threaten your joy. Take a look at what is robbing you of energy, wasting your time and threatening your sense of peace. Let us commit to a life-giving path, joining Suze and the battalion for truth. We can discover our own version of what it means to be both fierce and intentional. Meanwhile, I'm hoping for another spectacular Bahamas weekend with Suze and her company of friends—maybe when she turns 65...

—N.B.

BECAUSE I SAID SO: AN INTRODUCTION

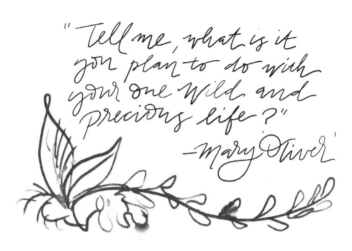

"Tell me, what is it you plan to do with your one wild and precious life?"

—Mary Oliver [1]

The following is a whole bunch of words, written mainly to my children—but you're more than welcome to read along. I've been jotting down ideas I have about the things I've been told, seen in a movie, read in a book, heard at church (ugh), or just generally absorbed—that are prevarications (which is a big word for a big fat lie) of what is actually true.

About me.

About these wild and beautiful children of mine.

About the world they live in.

But mostly, about the God who crazy loves all of the above.

Like a lot of Moms in the world, my mother used to say to me anytime I questioned her about anything—bedtime, snacks, wardrobe selections, and so much more—"Because I said so." My mom died a couple years ago, but in her nearly 84 years of living, there were many "Because I said so" moments between us. Mom had rules deeply ingrained in her, rules that helped her navigate what to her was a big, dangerous world. For me though, those rules would keep me, for years, from believing I could ever please her or even get close enough to her to gain all the benefits that come from being deeply intimate with one's Mom.

As I got older, I began to wake up to the fact that some of the ways I was living (people pleasing, not taking good care of my body, and trusting myself more than God, to name a few) were actually rooted in wrong thinking about my place in the world. I so desperately wanted to belong, to have a spot that was unequivocally mine, that I slowly but surely began to believe things that just weren't true. After enough years of living out of the falsehoods I was believing, that way of living began to stop working. I wasn't able to navigate my good but complicated life very well anymore. My mind, body, and spirit were beginning to take the toll of having a love affair with wrong thinking about my body, about my relationships, about my faith, and about what work I was called to, and so much more. So, in my 30s, I began to do some really important work that included talking to trusted friends, attending therapy, and journaling, all in the hope of breaking up with these lies and gaining more freedom, joy and truth in my life.

In the process, I discovered an important truth: my mom wasn't the only one shaping my identity with powerful untruths. My dad, my culture, my church, my workplace, every audition or try-out, every doctor's waiting room, and, of course, my own wrong thinking all helped in the construction of some pretty twisted approaches to my way of being in the world. I've believed lies about my worth and value, my health, my marriage, my relationships, my place in the world, and my faith that just aren't true, and I've spent much of my adult life trying to get untangled from some of this thinking. I hope you find not only your own story inside pieces of mine but also some encouragement to keep going, to keep looking for hope, to keep unraveling the lies you've been told. And by the end, maybe we'll both be experiencing more LIFE.

You'll see that I've identified some broader categories of the lies I've believed and lived out of over the years. Inside each of those sections is a truth offered that I've begun to live from instead, and then, some stories and thoughts from my own life offered as "evidence" for that more truthful way of living. All throughout, there are spots to do some reflecting on what you might think is true about your _____ (fill-in-the-blank lie from your own story), but it may not be. You'll then get a chance to scribble some thoughts about what the actual truth FOR YOU might be, and then follow that up with how you might live, think, act, and feel differently because of this discovery, and note for yourself who among your trusted people you will tell about this discovery (because change doesn't happen in a vacuum).

In all honesty, this is the only transformational path I've found: to identify the lie foundational to something I'm thinking, feeling, or doing, and then replace that lie with what's true (and by true, I mean actually True*). Then, figure out, through prayer and lots of listening to God, what I'm going to do with this discovery, and finally tell someone about it—someone who can hold me accountable.

That's right. Finally, actually DO something with my discovery.

The result? An opportunity to start living from a completely different place.

Thanks for picking these words up. I'm honored you would (even if you are one of the 28 members of my family who I arm-wrestled to read this).

Before we start, I'm mindful you may be asking, "Suze, why should I start digging around into my ways of thinking, feeling, and doing? I'm fine just the way I am, thank you very much."

Think about it this way: we don't fail in new ways. So, if you find yourself stepping into the same darn "hole" in your life, over and over again, you might want to consider if what you're thinking, feeling, or doing is based in Truth.

Honestly, the only thing I know to tell you is that poking and prodding into the lies you've believed and replacing them with the Truth you discover will invite you to MORE.

More you, more life, and more God.

And if that doesn't convince you, you should do it...

Because I Said So.

*By capitalizing the T in Truth, I'm referencing the kind of Truth the Bible speaks of (John 14:6). In other words, promises made that will stand the test of time and circumstances.

Part 1: The Body

the body

LIE

If you take care of your body, find the right diet, sleep enough, exercise appropriately, don't put anything toxic in it, you will never get surprised by anything going wrong in your mental or physical health.

TRUTH

Sometimes we get sick, can't conceive children, don't like what we see in the mirror, and are hard pressed to shake the trauma our bodies hold onto. This is not an indicator of whether we got "it" all exactly right, but rather a reflection of the brokenness all around us.

Much has been written lately about our bodies, the trauma that comes their way, and the subsequent pain we hold onto inside these fragile frames of ours. My body is no different than any other, except it has survived Cancer more than once and come out the other side with way fewer internal "parts" than I was born with. This body of mine spent years trying to create life. I conceived three, lost one, carried and delivered two dear lives after nearly a decade of being told I couldn't. My body has starved itself and then sought comfort in bag after bag of sour cream and onion chips. I have hated my body and I have treated my body with great tenderness.

For years I believed the lie that if I just took care of myself by eating right, getting enough sleep and exercise, and drinking enough water, both my mental and physical health would be just "fine." That has not been my story and based on conversations I have had with women young and old, it hasn't been their story either.

The truth is, sometimes our bodies let us down. We are broken people, living in a broken world and all that brokenness is going to have an impact on our physical forms. In a world full of rage and greed and isolation and some pretty seriously twisted thinking about what it means to be content with who we actually are, how could our bodies not respond?

My origin story, like yours, is that I was fearfully and wonderfully made. My belief is that from the moment we're born, we move further and further away from this truth. Part of that movement is believing lies about our bodies and how they are created. The evidence presented here explores the different lies I believed about my body, and the journey I've been on to untangle my thinking around those lies and to move, ever so slowly, back to that beautiful "fearful and wonderful" starting point.

So we're not giving up. How could we! Even though on the outside it often looks like things are falling apart on us, on the inside, where God is making new life, not a day goes by without his unfolding grace. These hard times are small potatoes compared to the coming good times, the lavish celebration prepared for us. There's far more here than meets the eye. The things we see now are here today, gone tomorrow. But the things we can't see now will last forever.

—2 CORINTHIANS 4:16-18 (The Message)[1]

EXHIBIT A: IT'S CANCER

When I was 15 years old, my parents and I returned from a spring break trip where I had managed to cook myself in the sun sufficiently enough that the entire top layer of my epidermis was peeling off.

In my defense, this was 1980, long before anyone was talking about skin Cancer or SPFs. Instead, we were slathering baby oil on our bodies, spraying lemon juice in our hair (trying to go blonde?) and rotating from front to back trying to get an even bake. As a high school freshman, I knew the greatest souvenir you could bring back from the beach was not a t-shirt—it was a golden brown tan. Dumb. I know, but hey, all the cool kids were doing it.

So, on this particular Sunday morning, I was once again applying lotion to my already peeling face (trying to maintain the bronze I had achieved until school on Monday) when I noticed in the mirror that my neck was swollen. My mom was on the phone giving my grandma all the scoop from the trip, the mail the neighbors had held for us was spread all over the kitchen table, and the week's worth of sandy laundry was piled in appropriate washing categories on the floor of the kitchen.

I walked over to my mother, pointed to my neck, and mouthed to her, "What do you think this is?" My mother would tell the story later, explaining how she knew immediately something was wrong. Deeply and profoundly wrong. First thing Monday morning, she scheduled a doctor's appointment for me and we began a marathon that for 42 years has been part of my story.

Now, I want you to know a little bit about my growing-up years. I was the youngest of three. My parents got married young and stayed married until they were old. I was raised with the understanding that 4 things really mattered:

My Faith
My Family
My Education
My Mother's Rules

I was a "good" kid and didn't really dabble in any of the other stuff some of my friends were experimenting with. No drugs, no smoking (except for that one time in 7th grade on the youth group trip to Kings Island), no alcohol, no missing curfew. However, I don't want you to think I was being driven by some deep, Godly conviction. The real reason why I didn't get into trouble as a kid? Please see #4 in the above list.

So, all that to say, the first 15 years of my life were pretty typical. Average midwestern upbringing—I was an athlete in an athletic family, an honor roll student in a family of people much smarter than I, a theater geek, and a class officer. I grew up in a solid Christian family where I was loved and protected by two parents who were deeply committed to each other and their three children.

So, picture me at 15, sitting in the doctor's office, hearing the doctor tell me and my parents, "It's Cancer" and watching my 6'2" father hit the floor in a dead faint, and you'll be right beside me at the exact moment I first questioned the idea that "clean living = good health." It wouldn't be the last time in my life I would consider that idea to be a lie.

That first diagnosis was Hodgkin's Lymphoma. Hodgkin's is a blood Cancer that is caused by a change in the DNA of a particular branch of white blood cells called B lymphocytes. And honestly, no one knows why the DNA tells the white blood cells to mutate, but they do, and the result is Cancer. The treatment I received for it has long been dismissed from the protocol, but back then, it's how the doctors made sure I was around to get my driver's license.

My second diagnosis came almost exactly a decade later, and at that time, Cancer showed up in my thyroid. I discovered the mass months before I ever spoke about it, because everyone knows something is not true until you say it is. I was married by then, so for this part of the adventure I had a teammate. While he kind of knew what he was signing up for when he asked me to marry him, I don't think anything really prepares you to hear that someone you love with all your heart has Cancer. We were young, broke seminarians, living in an apartment that was exactly big enough to cost us $82.00 a month.

My third diagnosis came another ten years later, and this time we caught the Cancer in its formative stages...twice. I had a full hysterectomy at 35 as well as a lumpectomy, both for pre-Cancerous tumors discovered by our beloved family physician, Dr. H. By then, there were three children in this family we call a tribe, and my unresolved trauma and grief and anxiety were catching up with me. With a seven, six, and two-year-old, there didn't seem room to go to the bathroom by myself, let alone deal with what it meant to have my life being chased down by Cancer again.

My fourth, and final so far, brush with the Big C came, you guessed it, another decade later, when I was 45. This time, Dr. H discovered a tumor on my pancreas. If you don't know much about your pancreas (I didn't), it's hidden behind about 4,000 body parts and in order to find out if it is or isn't Cancerous, you often have to have a surgery called the Whipple. The Whipple saved my life and wrecked it all at the same time. For me, this surgery would require four places where my innards had to be disconnected, the removal of one-third of my pancreas, and then, of course, four places of reconnection. I'll save you the messy details, but suffice it to say that my body and I now have a very complicated relationship with the bathroom.

A couple of years ago, I turned 55. The morning of my birthday I woke up early and in the stillness of the morning, I started running a body scan, thinking through all the possible places where Cancer might grow that year. Not a great way to start a birthday, but at the moment it seemed wise to do. I was three for three when it came to diagnosis on the "fives", and hope is costly. Honestly, I didn't feel I had it in me to take the risk required to hope that 55 would be the year that I would NOT hear "It's Cancer," from some doctor's mouth.

The year progressed and nothing happened. Well, lots happened—we did the things you do when you're living your life. We went to work. We navigated the impact of a global pandemic. We mourned the death of my mom. We sold the home we had raised our children in. We bought my parents' house and moved in with my Parkinson's-diseased dad. We loved each other and our family as best we knew how—and an entire year passed with no Cancer.

I'd love to tell you we jumped up and down and had a big party when I turned 56 and was Cancer-free.

However, there was a worldwide pandemic that had kind of worn us all down and honestly, there was also my own skepticism. There's an old saying about dogs chasing cars and the dog not knowing what to do when it catches said car...that's how I felt. I began to realize, as the months went on, that I knew how to be sick. I was familiar with being the "Cancer girl." I could navigate doctors and testing and waiting rooms and bad news with the best of them. But was I going to be able to NOT be "Cancer girl?" To live out from underneath that shadow of bad news was something I had begged God for, and now it was here and I wasn't sure what to do next.

We did celebrate that Cancer-free year. I turned 56 and there were balloons and steak and meaningful words about the impact of my life. I went to bed that night with a full heart and also a mind that was deeply aware I had some work to do around freedom and faith and what it means to live a hope-filled life.

Suffice to say, I have had a long and precarious relationship with my body and the way it works or doesn't. I have sought the counsel of wise physicians and supplemented where my body was lacking. I have exercised, prayed, fasted. I have eaten correctly, been anointed, and consumed 64 oz. of water a day.

And despite it all... Cancer.

Yet after all of that, here's what I know for sure: There really aren't any guarantees when it comes to my health.

But what there is, is plenty of Hope.

That costly commodity promised freely and completely in the person of Jesus.

I'm in my late 50s now. I am healthier, both mentally and physically, than I've been in a long, long time. I don't know if I'll get sick again, but I do know I have begun to see what this pattern of "not wellness" has been doing in my life. It has, over and over, tried to convince me that I was somehow responsible for my sickness, that it was my indulgence in food with too many preservatives, my drinking too much coffee (heaven forbid), my putting off exercising, or my persistent lack of faith that was causing it all.

Dr. H, that doctor of mine who has seen every nook and cranny of my fragile body, once told me that there's a theology to my biology. I love that and I think about it often. I don't understand it, really, but it has helped me find purpose in the suffering that has been mine. My body, my very being, is intertwined with the God who thought it was a good idea to make it—the same God who flung the stars into the night sky and carved the Grand Canyon out of the middle of no-where Arizona.

Yes, Cancer has been an unwanted and uninvited companion of mine for over forty years, AND, it has also been an oddly beautiful gift.

It has made me choose LIVING rather than just staying ALIVE, over and over and over again.

It has ingrained in me, deep into my bones, a particular kind of JOY that I'm not sure I could explain if I tried.

It has connected me to the One who made me, fearfully and wonderfully in the belly of that rule-making mother of mine and helped me see that even if I get it ALL right, something might still go wrong inside this fragile frame I walk around in. My relationship with illness has taught me I have everything I need to survive, again. It's all linked up—the living and the dying and the faithing. It's inte-grated, it's one, it's connected. My breathing and the One who gives me breath coexist within the mystery of being me, and nothing can break that connection.

This lie I've believed for a big portion of my life: If you just take care of yourself and by that I mean, if you eat right, get enough exer-cise, and make sure your sleep is sufficient, you will never get an un-wanted call from a doctor, I believe is also pervasive in our culture.

The problem with this way of thinking is what does any of it even mean today? For example, should I eat carbs or not? Should I cut refined sugar and dairy, or not? What about intermittent fasting or Keto—which one will work for me? Then there's working out? Am I a runner? A weightlifter? Should I focus on cardio or endurance? What is the appropriate number of times and the sufficient number of minutes to work out at the gym? Don't even get me started on sleep.

Eight hours or six hours—which is actually optimal? When does REM sleep kick in? Why do I wake up every morning at 3:00 a.m. to pee and then lay there for an hour worrying—that can't be good?

And so, whether I get that all sorted out or not, the reality is my body is fragile.

Everybody's is.

And sometimes, fragile things break. Sometimes the break can be repaired, sometimes not. Over the last 40+ years, I've been learning how to be OK with that. What I have discovered is this: it is often in the fragile places where the unbreakable love of God shines brightest.

When I had that Whipple surgery at 45, the recovery was long and complicated. I spent two weeks in the hospital and then recovered at home for another 10 weeks. I couldn't do much during that time, after all the rearranging of my insides. I had to relearn a lot of things about nutrition and make significant changes to my daily rhythms and routines. I had to learn what I could eat that my body would actually tolerate. It was a long road of trial and error as to how much water was too much water to drink with a meal. I spent a lot of time wondering if my stomach and my bowels would ever start getting along again. One of the first mornings I was home by myself, I found myself in the bathroom, again. I was in excruciating pain and doubled over on the toilet. I began praying, asking God to do something to bring relief.

As I prayed and cried, I thought of the Apostle Paul. Now, you might be thinking, that's a strange thing to be thinking of when you're in the predicament I was in, but actually it makes a ton of sense. Paul was the guy who, in one of his letters, wrote about an ongoing ailment that he's struggled with for years. Paul even shares

> "It is often in the fragile places where the unbreakable love of God shines brightest."

that he begged God to remove this ailment, which Paul called a "thorn" and God's response to Paul was that the grace that was coming was going to be enough for Paul to keep going. God even said that His power would be perfected through Paul's "thorn."

To be honest, when I was "head between my knees" begging God for help, I wasn't thinking about anything particularly spiritual happening in me, it was just like the "thorn" story passed through my mind like a ticker tape. All I wanted was for the pain to stop, but in that moment I heard God whisper into my spirit, "Suze, stop begging me now and see if you can praise me in spite of the pain."

When I look back at that morning, I see myself in our tiny little bathroom sobbing. Not because of the pain anymore, but because I was beginning to understand something that had always been true—God is worthy to be praised no matter how well my body is or isn't working in any given moment.

Paul also talks about a faith that allows us to delight in weakness and while I'm pretty sure I'm not quite at that kind of faith yet, after nearly six decades of living, I'm learning that two things can be true. I was fearfully and wonderfully made AND the world is a pretty broken place and maybe, because of that brokenness, we all have and will always have a "thorn" and maybe more than one. If I was making you a list of my physical "thorns," I would have to include Cancer and infertility and anemia and osteoporosis, and a variety of other things.

None of those things happened because I failed at taking care of myself. That's a lie after all. God didn't just look away while Cancer, and a host of her unwanted friends, slipped through the back door of my physical health and wrecked everything so I would be left to clean up that mess alone.

The truth is my journey, and yours, too, if you want it, is all about navigating through the broken bits and parts of this world we live in, some of which end up revealing themselves in our physical bodies. I don't have to sort it out, or even understand all of the why—that's something I stopped chasing a long time ago—for this to be true. What I do have to do is identify the lie for what it is and replace it with something that is true, like God is unable to forget about me and His love is greater than even the most broken parts of the world that my physical health might be reflecting in any given moment. There's freedom in that, a freedom for which I'm deeply and profoundly grateful.

TO CONSIDER

What lie have I believed about my body and the way it does (or doesn't) work?

What truth could replace this lie?

What will knowing this truth change about the way I'm living?

Because change isn't a solo undertaking, who, among my trusted friends can I tell about this discovery?

Exhibit B: More Than You Could Ask Or Imagine

Unlike lots of women I talk to, I did not spend my growing up years dreaming about becoming a Mom. Don't get me wrong, I had dolls I played with and later, plenty of my parents' friends to babysit for. However, I also had basketball and track, choir and drama, chores to get done, a summer job to hate, friends to keep up with, and boys to try and get to notice me. There just wasn't much room to dream about babies and "mom-ing." However, years later, becoming a mother seemed to be the furthest thing from reality due to my sickness. Holding a brand new, fresh-from-the-Maker-life would be all I could think about.

Babies weren't really a part of my childhood years. We didn't have younger cousins that I could commandeer at family gatherings and my parents were a little older when they had me, so their friends didn't have little ones either. Honestly, I can't really remember the first time I held a baby—I was probably 12 or 13 and most likely was terrified because some Mom and Dad, desperate for a night out, thought I was responsible enough to be in charge of their BRAND NEW PERSON. In addition to all of that, doing everything you could to not experience a teen pregnancy was a HUGE deal in my high school and in our culture at the time. After all, the lie was there: take care of yourself and nothing bad will happen to you or your body.

There was no reality show highlighting "teen moms" then, actually there were no reality shows at all. Instead, "unmarried teen mom" was a status our parents, teachers, youth group leaders, and the media treated as a pariah. A number of times, I overheard my Mom talking with a friend about someone's daughter, rarely the son, who had "gotten herself in trouble" (that always meant pregnancy, not grand theft auto) and now her life was "ruined."

Ruined.

That's a pretty big word especially for me, as a kid, to take in about pregnancy and what that might mean in a person's life.

We also didn't really talk a lot about how babies were made in our house. I had a general idea that I picked up from the "sex talk" in my 5th grade science class, and just to be clear, no actual talking about sex, intercourse, or lovemaking took place—that's just what the very dramatic 11 year olds were calling it. Overall, sex was a pretty foggy area for me and I had a lot of questions. Was this "activity" men and women did together just for the making of babies or was there another purpose? Was a girl's life really ruined if this happened to her? No one ever talked about the boy—would his life be demolished as well? How did it all work (as in, what parts went where and why)? To be clear, while I was confused about a lot, I was sure of one thing, this topic was not something to bring up at the supper table.

In the summer of my 4th grade year, a gentleman came to our door selling books. These weren't just any books. These were 32 beautifully bound green, white, and gold hardback tomes that contained everything there was to know, about anything, for all time ever. They were called the Encyclopedia Britannica. I remember my Mom and Dad talking for a long time about whether they should spend the $200.00 to make the purchase (equivalent to $1400.00 today) and when they decided "Yes!" because it was an "investment in their children's education," 10 year old me was pretty excited. When those gorgeous books were finally lined up on the bookshelf left of the fireplace and I had the letter "G" edition open in my lap, looking at pictures of the Grand Canyon and reading about the anatomy of a Grasshopper's body, you could not have convinced me that the salesman and those volumes of information weren't the greatest thing that ever happened to me.

So, two years later, when I "became a woman" and I had questions about what was ACTUALLY happening to me, because I couldn't remember a thing from that 5th grade "talk" and my mother was sitting atop her riding lawn mower cutting the grass, I went to the bookshelf, pulled off the letters "P" and "M" and starting researching. Sadly, it wasn't very helpful.

So, with all that in mind—a full childhood and youth, no real access to babies, the idea that a pregnancy could ruin a person, and very vague information from an it's-out-of-date-as-soon-as-you-print-it set of encyclopedias—reproducing myself was not something I spent much, if any, time daydreaming about.

And then, I got sick.

In my second surgery, for my very first Cancer, as the surgeon was taking organ samples and removing potential Cancer hosting organs and glands, he tucked my ovaries behind my uterus. He told my parents this was the only way he knew to give my reproductive system a fighting chance to be protected from the blasting my body was getting ready to endure. It was a lot to process for a 15 year old girl, who mostly just wanted to get back to her very average spot on the high school track team running hurdles.

I recovered, on the outside. But on the inside, my body would hold the trauma from that surgery for decades. It was like all my systems got hit with a control/alt/delete, and some of them had a difficult time rebooting. My reproductive system was one of those hit the hardest. From that point forward, my cycle was never "normal" and I found myself living with a new reality that would cause me decades of suffering, sadness, and sorrow.

I met Kelly Fair in the second semester of my freshman year of college, when I was 19. He was a funny, kind, big-hearted, brown-eyed guy who only made me want to be me. We went on our first date in the dead of Winter 1984 and were married by Summer of 1986. From the beginning, he has been my best friend and the safest place on earth for me. We were friends before we were anything else and one of the first things I told him was the secret I had been withholding from everyone else at the university: I had survived Cancer. As we got closer to knowing we wanted to spend our life together, I offered him the other untold truth I had buried inside me: there was a really good chance my body would never be able to create or carry life. This man handled both of those tellings like he would every other piece of difficult news our lives together would hand him—with a steadiness and depth of faith that has cost him dearly and yet has held our family in a state of stability and security for over 35 years.

We spent the first couple years of our marriage doing what most newlyweds do—getting to know each other, trying to figure out our money situation (we didn't have much), moving, getting a dog, learning how to shop for groceries, and trying to figure out our sex life. We were both virgins with very little dating experience and even less exploration and conversation about our sexual selves—it was all new, sometimes exciting, and sometimes scary territory for both of us.

By the end of year two, we decided we wanted to be parents and to start trying to get pregnant. Our thinking was that my body was a bit of a wild card as far as knowing whether it would or wouldn't be able to create a life and so we should get started as soon as possible. If I could go back and tell that dear, fragile, mostly broken 21-year-old me anything, it would be to "slow down." "Let your body and your mind and your heart come back to you before you try to make another human." Would I have listened to me? Probably not. Honestly, I was sure that a baby would fix so much that was still fractured inside my body and my spirit. Because in my early 20's I was still convinced that anything that was not working in my physical body was my fault. I had been too intense playing sports. I hadn't nourished myself correctly. I wasn't a "good" enough person (whatever that meant). These were all things I believed as time without a baby kept marching forward.

For the next six years, we did all we knew to do to try and conceive a brown eyed, dark-haired bundle of joy. We read books, we consulted doctors, we put miles and miles on our old ugly brown hand-me-down Buick Skylark traveling to the infertility center. I took my temperature and crazy expensive drugs. We placed pillows under my bum and I laid with my legs in the air for the prescribed post-sex timeframe. It all became very clinical and we began to grow further and further away from why we were doing this in the first place, and from each other.

And then, we got pregnant.

And then, we miscarried.

And then, I knew I couldn't go through all of that again.

We wanted to be parents more than we wanted to be pregnant, and honestly, we just couldn't fathom spending the money it would require to keep going on the infertility journey.

Side note: stopping was our choice, what was right for us. I believe in every journey that requires sacrifice and hope and disappointment and a "this may not work but we've got to try" way of thinking, there's a threshold where the people on the journey (and only them) will know when they're supposed to keep going or pause or just stop.

In all those years of trying to get pregnant, life kept happening around us and we wanted to rejoin it. We wanted our world to expand beyond the kind of hope that becomes enslaved to the monthly arrival of my period. We had friends, family, a dog, and work that needed our attention. Kelly was in grad school and I was working full time at a publishing house. Life went on.

In time, we began to think about adoption.

Almost exactly 12 months after the death of our first baby, as I was standing at the copy machine at work making copies of a letter we were going to send out in our Christmas card, asking everyone we knew to help us on our adoption journey, I found out that the cousin of a co-worker was pregnant with a baby she would not be able to parent. Our hearts were ready, our spirits had healed (mostly), and so we jumped into action. We wrote letters, completed a home study, called our lawyer, made contact with the birth mother's caseworker, and got my parents to cosign a loan with us. We dared to hope again, that we would be chosen and become parents after all.

She did choose us. Oh, the joy.

Then she un-chose us. Oh, the despair.

That back and forth continued until I told the caseworker we weren't doing well with the roller coaster ride, so please just call us when her decision was final.

On February 6, 1993 I was at work, probably back at the copier, and our department secretary told me I had a phone call from Michigan. It was the caseworker and her words would be the kind of declaration that changes lives. It sure did mine: "Hey Suze, I just wanted to let you know your son was born this morning." When I hung up the phone and turned around, my entire department was standing behind me, hanging over the walls of my cubicle. When they saw my face, the celebration started.

I called Kelly and the greatest adventure of our lives, being parents together, began.

Benjamin Scott Fair wouldn't come home for another six weeks and his adoption wouldn't be final for another six months, but from the moment I heard he was ours, the thing I never thought I wanted and then wanted more than anything—Motherhood—was happening. I naively thought this longing had died along with the first pregnancy, but the news of Benjamin brought about a flourishing inside me again; I was going to be someone's Mom, and this "someone" was already spectacular. I didn't have to create and carry him inside me for that to be true.

We met our son for the first time when he was nearly seven weeks old and from the first moment we stepped into that foster home and I scooped him up into my arms, a healing began inside me that would unravel a knot I had tied myself up in starting when I was 15 years old. All I know now, though, was that the first time I looked into those dark brown eyes and gently held his head full of dark wavy hair in my hands, God began to teach me something that He's still teaching me today: His plans are always better than mine.

Ben's birth-mom wasn't a teenager when she got pregnant with him. She was in her 30s and already had six children from a marriage that didn't carry her into her middle years. She had already been mothering for years and knew, in the season of life when she was pregnant with him, she did not have what she needed to parent this new baby. Her name was Sharon and to this day, this woman remains my hero, one of the bravest people I'll never meet but I see often when I look into our son's eyes. For the first several years of Ben's life, I sent her a letter and a picture via her caseworker. Never knowing if she received them, my hope was that even if just one got to her, her heart would be blessed and her spirit at rest—she had chosen well. We loved this boy as she did, deep and wide. 25 years later, I would find out that Sharon had received at least one of those letters, because she had his one-year-old picture in her Bible, as a placeholder—for what I'll never be able to ask her because she died in 2017.

Someone told me once that it was important for me to remember that in order for my family to begin, some part of someone else's family had to die. Maybe that's the "ruining" those worried mothers talked about all those years ago. When the plans that have been carefully laid down for your life are radically changed by the beginnings of a miraculous, and yet possibly unexpected, new life making his way into the world, it can feel like a hard left turn in a road that once seemed straight and true. We're still going to reach our destination, just maybe not the one we were planning on.

"Because the truth is, sometimes our bodies can't seem to do what other people accomplish with very little effort. This reality has nothing to do with whether we followed all the rules, or we are less favored by God, or whether we have some unknown sin in our lives."

If all that's true, both of us, Sharon and I, were "ruined" and we were both ready to mother Benjamin in the most loving way we knew. One by relinquishing and the other by gathering up and holding close.

My journey as a Mom has been more than I could have ever asked for or imagined. Full of both great joy and real heartache. Ben doesn't get credit for all that good and bad—he's got two sisters who showed up later to help him share that load.

For me, believing the lie that if I just took care of myself then I would never be surprised by how my body was or wasn't working, wasn't an option anymore. By the time I miscarried and we adopted Ben, I had already had Cancer twice and been through years of infertility treatments. I was no longer surprised by my body's inability to function correctly. What I had to learn how to do, in order to not get drawn down into the abyss of despair which I was often tempted by, was to decide again and again, that no matter what was happening on the inside of me, God was working out a really good plan for all of me. For whatever reasons only God is aware of, I got to be a mom. It didn't come to me in the "regular" way the first time. Sharon's choice and Benjamin's arrival made me a mother, completely separate from anything my broken body could or couldn't do.

Because the truth is, sometimes our bodies can't seem to do what other people accomplish with very little effort. This reality has nothing to do with whether we followed all the rules, or we are less favored by God, or whether we have some unknown sin in our lives. For the record, these are all things people told me when we were unable to conceive. No, sometimes our bodies don't work the way we think they should because that is the story that is ours to live. The Bible tells me that God is making all things new and I believe that's happening right now and it will keep happening both in my body and in the world around me. So, until it's ALL new, my deepest longing is to remain grateful for this life that is mine, which more and more is more than I could have ever asked or imagined.

TO CONSIDER

What lie have I believed about my ability to create life (whether that's a child or health or some other form of beauty)?

What truth could replace this lie?

What will knowing this truth change about the way I'm living?

Because change isn't a solo undertaking, who, among my trusted friends can I tell about this discovery?

Exhibit C: It's Ok, You Can Let Go Now

I'm going to say something now that you know, but you may have forgotten: our bodies are intricately woven together, miraculous-beyond-belief-that-they-even-kind-of-sort-of-work things of beauty. It doesn't matter the shape or size or age or pigment of our skin—these things we walk around in are ridiculously amazing and complicated.

And confusing.

Sometimes, very confusing.

What starts out seemingly perfect, healthy, and whole can, in an instant, break, either temporarily or permanently. Normal pregnancies sometimes result in unexpected "differences" or loss. Routine procedures can develop complications and nothing is ever the same again. Expected aging happens and our biology begins the process of wearing out, sometimes causing us pain and frustration.

This beautiful frame of skin and muscle and bones and organs and nervous systems will bring us the kind of pleasure we will never have words for, and sorrow that is so profound we often carry it with us forever.

My body, the whole of me, has experienced all of that beauty and every bit of that grief and I'm convinced it all still resides somewhere inside me. All of that joy and lots of that pain. I believe our bodies hold onto so many things: experiences, smells, emotions, and memories so old we thought we forgot. Like, seeing the ocean for the first time or holding your child while they are brand new to you. As well, the body can hold difficult and dark things, like being harmed by a trusted someone or watching a loved one die or walking the road of a life-altering diagnosis. One of the most profound challenges of my life has been to identify where both the pain and the joy dwell inside me and do the work of releasing whatever might be causing me harm.

I grew up spending the summer at my family's lake home. My

parents moved us all there on Memorial Day and we didn't move back to our "town" home until Labor Day. We were outside constantly and played in the water every day. Most days, after our chores were done, Mom would get us three kids in the boat and she would drag us around on some sort of water apparatus (water skis, an inner-tube, trick skis, paddle board—you name it, we rode it). It was a pretty great way to grow up. I was bribed, with a dollar, into learning how to ski the summer I was five. By the time I was nine I was slaloming. I'm only saying this to share that skiing was, for me, like riding a bike for other children. I started young and did it a lot. As I got older, I didn't ski every day, but still did it frequently enough that my muscles quickly remembered how to do it and could easily get back in the flow.

The summer I was 35, after that particularly tough winter because of my third brush with Cancer, I arrived at summer determined to prove I still had "it." I was going to ski. So, we loaded up the kids, jumped in the boat with my dad driving and I attempted to do what I had done literally hundreds of times for the past 30 years of my life.

But, for reasons I never could figure out, I could not get up, and on my fifth or sixth attempt, I felt, and heard, something "pop" in my left hip. I couldn't get in the boat and I later could barely walk. I found out later that I had stretched, nearly to the point of tearing, my hamstring. It was incredibly painful, both physically and emotionally (I was after all attempting to be the cool Mom in front of my kids).

Three years after the injury, I was speaking at a women's conference. After the last session ended, this woman who I had not met came up to me and asked, "When did you injure your left hamstring?"

I'm sorry, "What?"

As we talked, she told me she was a massage therapist and she could tell by the way I was standing and how I favored that leg that I had sustained an injury—probably a hamstring tear. My body had been holding onto that pain for over 1000 days and it was showing. Luckily, there was someone paying attention. She was amazing, asked me if she could work on me, laid me down on the floor of that meeting room and provided the kind of relief I hadn't felt since the day I had attempted to water ski.

When I was a kid, there weren't a lot of conversations happening about "processing your pain," and so I encountered that first Cancer diagnosis with minimal tools in my emotional toolbox. As the wounds started to come, I wasn't quite sure what to do with all the feelings about them and so, I did very little. I got told I would miss a sleepover because my health was just too fragile and I was disappointed, but it made sense, so what do you do with the disappointment? I was in the hospital opening night of my play, which was so very sad and I was also kind of angry, but where do those feelings go when you're where you're supposed to be—fighting for your life? My period stopped after all the treatment was over and I became deathly afraid I would never have children, but who do I tell about that when I'm 15 and the goal is "stay alive," not worry about some future unknown children? It happened over and over, big emotions would come and I wouldn't know what to do with them so I just held onto them. For me, it was a little like pulling a hot dish out of the oven with a too-thin oven mitt and frantically looking for a place to set it down and with no option available, just standing there holding the hot pan instead. All the while, I can feel the blisters forming on my hands.

What I know now is that when I got diagnosed the first time my parents were doing the best they knew with what they had. Unfortunately, they didn't know much about what to do with that kind of traumatic event and so, because there didn't seem to be anywhere to put that pain, I held onto it for too long and eventually, some of it just ended up buried inside me. Remember that old song, "One Bad Apple" by the Osmonds (I had a big Donnie Osmond crush—don't judge)? The chorus of the song said, "One bad apple won't spoil the whole bunch, girl." Well, that's pretty much a lie. Over time, a bad "anything" will spoil everything it comes in contact with.

That's how it's been for me at least—and as I got older, I became aware I had some "bad" thinking around things attached to my body and its health. I was struggling to trust my body to do what it was supposed to do—as in, stay healthy, create life, be beautiful, and not die young. Because of unresolved pain and grief connected to my illness, I began to believe that something that breaks once, like the cellular makeup and its ability to make Cancer, will be broken forever. There didn't seem to be any room for hope or grace or redemption when it came to the physical body that was me.

So many smarter and more educated people than me are talking about this idea of buried pain, for which I'm grateful. What I know is that trauma, if left unacknowledged or unprocessed, will eventually reveal itself in our bodies. Like my stretched and wounded hamstring, our pain, no matter how high the shelf we've put it on, will somehow, someway make itself known. My job as the one who walks around in this beautiful and sometimes broken gift of a body is to pay attention to how that might be happening.

Often, our bodies are asking us for something—a nap, a meal, a couple pain relievers, a vacation, some attention, a glass of water, a doctor's insights—and we are the only ones who can give it what it's asking for. Unfortunately, if we're not paying attention to the signs, we won't be able to offer ourselves the much needed resource.

"This beautiful frame of skin and muscle and bones and organs and nervous systems will bring us the kind of pleasure we will never have words for, and sorrow that is so profound we often carry it with us forever."

These days I'm pretty dialed into what my body needs and yet, I'm confident I still miss plenty of my body's signals for help. Whether it's denial or the pace I'm living or just an unwillingness to stop, I have caused harm to myself because I haven't wanted to look past the thing my body is presenting to me. For instance, I have had a lot of pain in my neck and shoulders over the years. For a long time I said that this kind of pain was because I was stressed or tired. While sometimes that's true, now I know that my body might be trying to tell me something with the pain and it's important to get to the "thing behind the thing." As in, am I just stressed or tired, or am I in pain because of an old wound or trauma that is trying to come to the surface? For lots of people, neck and shoulder pain is just stress or fatigue, for me the deeper cause of that neck and shoulder pain might be attached to the fact that when I was a teenager, my neck was cut open to remove a seven inch tumor.

In her book, *The Wisdom of Your Body*, Dr. Hillary McBride says it this way:

> "Our bodies are telling the stories we have avoided or forgotten how to hear. Sometimes our inability to feel our feelings (the earliest form of communication to arrive, and often the most shamed) means our bodies have to scream in order to get some attention. This can come in the form of illness, overwhelming emotion, or pain." [2]

Pain rarely looks or feels the same for people. Plenty of people I know ignore a sore throat, a mild fever, exhaustion, or a little anxiety, and instead they decide to push through to the next thing. I was one of those people for years and then, I learned that an odd response is most likely an old response.

So, when something starts to feel "off," either physically, spiritually, or emotionally, I've learned to ask myself, "is this old or new?" Am I responding to something that happened long ago or an interaction I just had? The distinction, for me, has proven to be very important as I navigate the art of pulling up old, unprocessed pain and do the work of letting it go and moving forward.

For the whole of my adult life, I have been afraid of big dogs. If I'm out on a walk and a big dog starts barking somewhere, anywhere, I go into high alert. The dog can be on a leash, fenced into the yard, or standing behind a screen door and I'm still terrified. If a big dog starts coming at me, game over—I will freeze, yell, just generally panic. Where did this fear come from? For years, I had no idea. I would ask my mom about it; it was such a powerful reaction, surely there must have been something that happened, somewhere in my childhood, with a big dog. She had absolutely no memory of anything. Trust me, I asked her about it MANY times. Finally, just a couple years ago I said something in front of my older sister. I had just gotten back from a walk and was still a little rattled from a run-in with the neighbor's overly "friendly" off-leash Boxer, and my sister said, "You're afraid because you got chased down the street by a big dog when you were probably 3 or 4." And just like that, all the years of doing whatever I could to avoid encountering a big dog made sense. My mind hadn't been able to access the memory, but my body sure did. Since then, I'm still aware that I don't trust big dogs, but I'm careful when I'm out on a walk, I make myself take my niece's giant Great Dane on a walk so I can live to tell the story, and I try to not completely retreat when I hear a big dog barking in the vicinity. I can do that because now I know why I'm afraid—I finally have a place to put the trauma. The buried fear got revealed by my sister's remembering, proving that revelation is an invitation to healing.

I'm deeply aware that there are many who carry their own deep and dark wounds. Not the being chased by a dog kind of wound, but the over and over-ness of sexual abuse, the blasting of verbal or physical assault, or the pain of a scary diagnosis that seems to follow them for years. All this causes a big emotional reaction that if we don't name it, feel it, and then process it, it will bury itself inside of us, hoping not to be heard from ever again. My story, however, would say that it just might bubble back up to the surface. For me, it affected how I held my body, a literal pain in the neck, and the things (big dogs, getting sick again, dying) I was afraid of.

There's an old saying that asks, "Why do bad things happen to good people?" Well, I decided long ago that assuming bad things won't happen to good people is just buying into the lie that if we just do all we can do to get it right (diet, sleep, exercise, etc.) then our bodies will work in tip top shape and never surprise us. These days, I'm spending more time wondering what might happen if I could lay that lie down and turn toward the truth instead. The truth that God made me to be whole and complete, and when I start to feel fractured or scattered, I need to pay attention to those feelings and ask if this could be an invitation to see if there might be some kind of old hurt that needs to be taken out and looked at.

Maybe in the looking, I'll discover that I can take another step toward wholeness where before there had only been something broken.

TO CONSIDER

What hurt have I hidden inside my mind or heart?

How has that hidden hurt affected me physically?

What lie have I believed about this pain? What truth could replace this lie?

What will knowing this truth change about the way I'm living?

Because change isn't a solo undertaking, who, among my trusted friends can I tell about this discovery?

EXHIBIT D: WELL DONE, YOU

There is a lie about a woman's body so pervasive that I have yet to meet a woman who hasn't had to deal with it. That lie says there is a body type that sets the standard for beauty and if you can get your body to look like that standard, all will be well in your life.

The problem is, that standard keeps changing and the formula to achieve it keeps morphing too. Like an ever moving target, we go on a quest to find just the right diet, the right amount of exercise, to drink the right amount of water every day, and get the required number of hours of sleep in a night in order to look a certain way. For years I have chased that standard and every time I didn't achieve it, I have had contempt for myself, often lamenting, "What's wrong with me?" The truth is there is nothing inherently "wrong" with me or the way my body looks. However, I didn't understand that until I was able to accept my body with all her scars and flaws. To accept her when she's 50 pounds heavier than the ideal for her height and age, or when she's 20 pounds underweight because of fall-out from a health crisis. Beauty is me, just as I am today. I know that's true because beauty has very little to do with what I see reflected in the mirror or in a magazine.

I have a secret dream, and it's not just for me. It's for every woman in my life that I have met or will meet. Actually, it's my dream for every female type person everywhere: I long for the day when the women I know can stand completely naked in front of a full-length mirror with good lighting and not have contempt for one single cell that is reflected back to them. No criticism about the extra weight, the wrinkles, the "pooch," cellulite, boobs, hair, face, any of it. In this dreamworld of mine, when I stand there and look at myself, all I will be able to see is everything she IS, not the list of the things she's not.

I'm sure there's a similar dream for the men in our culture, I've just never been one—so I'm not familiar with the crap they think about when they look in the mirror.

As a woman in the West, I'm not sure how we can avoid the images and expectations coming our way concerning what it means to be "pleasing" and that's been true for a while. Advertisers figured out a long time ago if they held up an ideal of anything, humans would want it. It works for vehicles, toothpaste, cookware, and how our bodies look. The reason they don't stop, even though there's been lots of conversation and controversy connected to body negativity and positivity, is because it works. We shake our fist about the objectification of a woman's body to sell cheeseburgers and then we click the link on an influencer's social media platform and buy the jeans she's wearing, hoping we too will also look hip and cool and thin.

Lest you think I'm casting stones, I am not. I have gotten caught in the cycle of longing for a version of me that looks more appealing to someone, somewhere that I've never met. I feel like it's like a hamster wheel of shame that I got on when I was an early teen and my hormones failed to fire in my mammary glands (AKA: cup size AA) and it has kept me spinning for the whole of my life.

I have had seasons when I deeply loved my body. As an athletic kid, I was always grateful that my body was strong and I could do all the running and jumping necessary to be a part of those teams. As an angsty teenager, I hated my body. My thighs were too big (from all that running and jumping), I was too tall, I had feet that were too big, and those dratted small boobs again.

Then I got sick for the first time, and my relationship with my body changed forever. I stopped trusting it to do the basic stuff, like have a period every 28-30 days, tell me when something was "off," be able to grow and maintain hair where hair belongs, and return to a healthy weight when the time was right. I have had such contempt for my body because of its weakness, for years believing a stronger body wouldn't have allowed Cancer cells to grow.

I have mistreated my body. I have underfed it, put it through the brutality of using laxatives to stay thin, over-exercised it, and completely ignored it when it was asking me for rest. I have also loved my body tenderly. Stretching it and making it strong, providing the nutrition it needs to stay well, learning how to rest for more than an afternoon, and drinking lots of water.

My mom had what they call an hourglass figure—ample bustline, small waist, and hips to match the bust. As previously alluded to, my shape was not the hourglass, it was more like an upside down margarita glass, narrow at the top and good "childbearing hips" (that's a direct quote from my high school drama teacher) on the bottom.

When I was about 13, and I was still waiting for the aforementioned barely noticeable boobs to show up, I was standing in my bedroom, staring fully clothed in the mirror at myself wondering about how I looked in the outfit I had chosen for the day. Unbeknownst to me, my mother was standing in the doorway watching me and from her vantage point she made what I'm confident she thought would be a helpful suggestion, "Let's get you a nice padded bra."

"Excuse me, what? Have we given up all hope of these things emerging? I mean I'm only 13 years old, I'm sure they will be here any day now." I didn't say any of that out loud, instead I just stood there stunned and embarrassed.

Every time I think about that moment, all I can remember is meeting her eyes in my mirror and feeling

"Beauty is me, just as I am today. I know that's true because beauty has very little to do with what I see reflected in the mirror or in a magazine."

such a deep sense of shame. As she explained why she made her comment, "It will balance out your figure and your clothes will look better," I couldn't even hear her through the humiliation. I'm pretty confident I told her "no way" and to "please get out of my room." Which she did, and I was left staring at the mirror, alone with what I viewed as "lack" in my mother's eyes. It would be the first time, but not the last, I would give in to the thinking that if my body just looked like it was supposed to, my mom would like me more. Mom liked me plenty, but in that moment my feeling of not measuring up to her standards was so strong that I interpreted it as lack of approval of me, my personhood, my essence—me.

So, you see long before the illness came, I was in a mini war with my body and the image I held of it.

Seven months after we brought Benjamin home from foster care, I realized I had missed my period. I was so caught up in the mothering of our little guy, going back to work, and still trying to figure out how to be a pastor's wife—for the first time in what seemed a million years, I wasn't paying attention to my cycle. Then, as I checked in with my body, I realized my boobs were tender and a cup of coffee hadn't sounded good for a couple of weeks. I was pregnant. Again.

However, my beloved husband didn't believe me and when I described to him how my body was feeling. He told me to put the baby down for a nap and he would run to the pharmacy, pick up a pregnancy test, and "prove to you that you're not pregnant." I'm sure his need to verify that I was not expecting was connected to a lot of hope and a little bit of "are you kidding me right now?" We had, after all, spent the last eight years of our life in infertility treatment and had literally, six months earlier, brought our son home. So, when those two lines showed up bright pink, the only response he could utter as we were both crammed into our tiny bathroom, so we wouldn't wake the baby, was "holy shit."

That entire pregnancy, I struggled to trust my body. Would it be able to carry this baby to term? Would he/she be safe inside me? Was all the stress and anxiety I was feeling transferring into the womb? I was in therapy at the time, with a brilliant woman named Linda. She had gently guided me through the miscarriage, the process of adopting Ben, and was doing the same as we awaited the arrival of this miracle baby who seemed to be doing just fine inside what I had long viewed as a broken body. I was so scared. I would often come to my sessions with Linda crying before she ever asked me a question. Because here's what was true for me in that season: while I was deeply grateful for the chance to be Ben's mom and felt connected to him in ways I thought only biologically possible, my longing to be pregnant and experience the miracle that is giving birth had never subsided. I think my tears in counseling and my worry in just the

everydayness of the pregnancy was tied to a simple, yet very complicated for me, hope: was my body going to be able to do this thing I
so badly desired?

On the first of July, 1994, I woke up coughing, so hard it felt like
I was going to hack up a lung. I was 39 weeks pregnant, 52 pounds
heavier than I had been when I peed on the stick in that tiny bathroom, and I was still wobbly about how this pregnancy was going to
end. After two days of sleeping in a chair so I could breathe, I called
the OBGYN's office and upon hearing my voice, which sounded like
I'd been smoking cigars (which I had not), they told me to come in.
My doctor wasn't available, but I met with her Nurse Practitioner,
who listened to my breathing and prescribed a safe decongestant
and sent me home. The morning of July 5th, I got a call from my doctor. She said, "Suze, I just can't get you off my mind. I was getting
ready this morning and couldn't stop thinking about you, so I think
you should come see me today." I trusted this woman. She knew my
whole story and had already had to tell me once in our history together that the child I was carrying was dead—she wasn't taking any
risks this time. So, Kelly and I dropped Ben off at the babysitter and
drove the 45 minutes to Dr. Beck-Coon's office. After listening to my
breathing and checking my lungs, she calmly told me that I needed
an X-Ray because she was worried about pneumonia. Her worry was
confirmed, I had pneumonia in both lungs and was admitted into
the very last room, at the end of the maternity hallway. We weren't
prepared for that; we did have the prerequisite "hospital bag" in the
trunk of the car, but we didn't have a plan for Ben or the dog or really
much else. We called my folks and gave them a list of things to pick
up, starting with Benjamin, and then asked them to swing by so we
could love on him a little and try to explain to his little 17-month-old
self what was happening.

That never happened. Because about a half hour after we got off
the phone with Mom and Dad, I said to Kelly, "I think I'm in labor." He
just looked at me like a deer in the headlights and said, "let me get
somebody." I was right. I had coughed that poor baby into position
and she was ready to come out. At 7 p.m., with just her dad, a nurse,

Dr. Beck-Coon, and me of course, to witness it—Katharine Elizabeth Fair made her speedy entrance into the world. My body had done it. While I felt like I had crawled my way to the finish line, we made it.

In the hours that followed the birth, I was very sick. The pneumonia was waging war in my lungs and the energy my body expended to give birth had cost me. I would end up spending eight days in the hospital and because of a very kind pediatrician, Katie got to stay with me.

That entire season—finding out we were pregnant, the 40 weeks of the pregnancy, the illness in my body, the birth, the hospital stay—changed me profoundly. Not just the mothering part, although that was amazing and challenging all at the same time. It was something else. Something deeper. Everytime I would hold Katie in those first months, I would think, "My body did that." Looking back, this was the beginning of me making peace with my biology, something I thought I would never be reconciled with. The work of me learning how to trust my body would be with me for a very long time and the learning would come with the help of wise counsel and time. I would discover that trusting my body was my choice. I no longer could say, out of hand, "My body can't do that." Instead now I had evidence that it could and I would get to choose, or not, to believe that reality.

When Ben was four and Katie was three, all those pregnancy signs and symptoms showed up again. This time, when I looked at Kelly across the heads of our running-around-like-crazy-people-children and said, "I'm pregnant," he believed me. Another crazy, miraculous gift. This pregnancy would prove to be uneventful, normal even—I gained a bunch of weight, peed a little bit every time I coughed, and had a craving for salami, pickles, and cheese (thus the weight gain). All that normalcy was a gift and I received it as such. At the end of a very long and hot July 1998, Mackenzie Ruth Fair arrived on the scene. Once again I held in my arms the evidence that my body was capable of so much more than just being sick.

One year after Mackenzie was born, I had my third run-in with Cancer. Remember that year I turned 35? In a short window of time, I had a pre-Cancerous lump removed from my left breast, several

Cancerous moles removed from my chest, and that full hysterectomy because of a pre-Cancerous mass found in my uterus. I remember thinking, "here we go again," but this time I had three children in my heart and my care and there was no time or desire to believe my body wouldn't fight. There would be no turning on myself this time. I chose to believe that while my body had brokenness in it it was also more than capable of performing miracles. This doesn't mean I never worried about my health during this year, it just means I was starting to make peace with the sometimes tangled up biology of me.

Through all this long and complicated, both loving and hateful, relationship with my body, what remains is a tenuous acceptance of the physicality of me in the here and now. It has taken me years of therapy, which I highly recommend by the way, and hours of journaling and a handful of trusted friends who know my whole story, to get to the place where I can practice the discipline of not lamenting what "was" or wishing for "would could be," but rather, what is true now.

Over and over I have been tempted to give into the world's version and view of what beauty is. When I look in the mirror and see something other than that, instead of running toward the latest diet fad or frantically hitting the gym, I've learned to push pause. I work to get to what's actually happening when I feel insecurity connected to what my body looks like. In addition, if my body has an ache or pain, I have been known to do one of two things: hide it and pretend it's not there or get overly dramatic about it and end up with both myself and the people I love stressed out. Instead, I've learned to pay attention to my body, check in with it often, go to the doctor regularly, and make sure I am authentically living in the healthier space that exists somewhere between "Nothing's wrong" and "The sky is falling."

Will I get sick again? I have no idea. Are the wrinkles taking over my face? Yes, but that's because I spent way too much time on the end of the pier for that NOT to be true. My energy is still strong, but my knees are starting to do that gravelly sound when I walk up the stairs. My left pinky ring hurts from the arthritis and I have long given up hope on going up a cup size in my bra. Sometimes my heart beats in a strange rhythm and I wonder if the damage done by the radiation treatment that saved my life all those years ago has messed up my heart for "normal" now. Even amidst all those unknowns and changes, I do know this one thing: I have a part to play in loving myself well and the key to that is staying grounded and present in the "now."

I don't know if I'll ever stand in front of that mirror naked as a newborn with zero judgment, but what I will do is pay attention to my body, offering it what only I can give it: care, rest, and a fighting chance for health. Which will allow me to look in the mirror, clothed or not, and say to that amazing human looking back at me, "Well done you."

Oh, and P.S.: my mother never gave up on the padded bra. When I was in my early 40s, she and I were shopping in a large department store and as we wandered into the women's undergarment section, my 70-something mother called out to the clerk across the way, "Where might we find the padded bras for the small breasted women?" Still felt the shame, but this time I could just turn and walk away, and I had the car keys, so she had to follow.

TO CONSIDER

What lie about my body is keeping me from living at peace with it, no matter the age, shape, size or level of health?

What truth could replace this lie?

What will knowing this truth change about the way I'm living?

Because change isn't a solo undertaking, who among my trusted friends can I tell about this discovery?

PART 2: FAITH

LIE
God's love can be earned, all I have to do is accept Jesus into my life, learn and then follow all the rules of being a "good" Christian, and don't mess up.

TRUTH
God invites us into an intimate, transformative, grace-filled relationship. Our "job" is to pursue it and Him and then tell others about it.

I became a Christian when I was 12 and I became a disciple when I was 42. If you're wondering what was happening in that 30 year gap, it was mostly all the things "good" Christians do to live the way they think they're supposed to, in order to get the life I thought was mine to take. I went to church, I read my Bible, I attended and led Bible studies, and yet, I often went to bed thinking, "If I die tonight, where will I end up?" and as I got older, that question morphed into, "Shouldn't there be more to this living by faith thing?" My life was crammed full of activities and yet, I honestly, felt very little. I went through a long season of spiritual blandness.

I had learned how to be busy DOING for God, and yet remained kind of horrible at BEING with God. The chapters coming ahead are some thoughts I have about the fact that we can't earn our way to the life we think we're promised. That life is already available to us, we just need to practice the discipline of listening to God first (that's our relationship with God) and then doing what He says (those are our responsibilities for the Kingdom). Understanding this connection between BEING and DOING is without fail, embedded in our understanding of who God is. If I don't know who God is, how can I know what kind of life He's actually called me to live? God cares about a lot of things I rarely think about, which is kind of sad if I ponder it for too long. But more than sad, it's a dilemma there's a solution for: greater and deeper faith.

> *"I had learned how to be busy DOING for God, and yet remained kind of horrible at BEING with God."*

The evidence presented here offers a response to the lie that God's love can be earned and if you're a well behaved Christian, and you don't make mistakes, you'll get rewarded. That's not how it works with God, the blessings in our life aren't proof that we had the right amount of faith or believing enough. The truth is God loves us deeply. Loves us so much that he invites us into a personal relationship with him so our lives can be transformed forever by that love.

"You can't know, you can only believe—or not."

—C.S. LEWIS[1]

Exhibit A: God Who?

I did not grow up with a clear grasp of who God is or how to get close to Him. As I look back at my understanding of the Divine, my relationship with Him, and what was true about me because of that relationship, I am pretty confident I was clear on the basics. If one accepted Jesus into her heart, followed the rules, went to church, and stayed out of trouble—all would be well. What I didn't have a clear understanding of were some of the nuances of loving and being loved by God.

I grew up in a household with two parents who loved each other and loved me and my siblings deeply. They were Christians who had grown up in homes with Christian parents, and so we three were raised to attend church every Sunday, read our bibles, pray, and learn the hymns of the church. I always knew my parents considered their faith a priority. We were taught to look out for the underdog, be generous with our resources, and make sure we were investing in the church. When we stayed with my paternal grandparents, we went to their little country church on Sundays and attended Vacation Bible School there in the Summer. I also grew up hearing stories about my mom's family and their participation in the church. However, all that generational belief and spiritual activity doesn't necessarily mean there was clarity on who God actually was and how a personal connection with Him worked.

Because I wasn't talking about God intimately or personally anywhere, God took on an almost mythological status. I was pretty sure God wasn't the same as the Easter Bunny or Santa, but did I really KNOW it as fact? Not quite. So, I began to think about God like many children do with big fantastical figures and he became someone to write a wishlist to or make three wishes on. I also began to transfer the way my parents treated me onto my understanding of how God might treat me or feel about me or think about me. Consequently, I spent the majority of my childhood believing that God's love was a love that needed to be earned and his approval could be gained by my achievements. As well, I was taught that it was one thing to accept Jesus into my heart, but what really mattered, and actually received more attention and conversation, were the rules of being a "good" Christian and how to live by them.

Over time I became quite skilled at learning how to offer my "talent, time, and treasure" for God and God's work, in order to earn that Godly love and approval. All the while, I didn't really know how the core concepts of a personal, intimate relationship with God worked. I left my childhood and stepped into adulthood clueless as to how faith, grace, mercy, forgiveness, justice, and peace were the true framework of my faith and that I really only had one assignment—to love the Lord with my whole being and stop leaning so hard on my own understanding of things.

In order to learn a new thing, sometimes you have to unlearn the old thing. For me it has required one step of faith after another to set aside the belief that I could earn anything (love, approval, forgiveness) from God and just receive what is so freely offered (grace, peace, truth, acceptance, etc.). Those steps of faith have been fueled by the love of a long-suffering husband, a trusted community of like-minded friends, time all by myself with a pen and a journal, and a gifted therapist. The very first step I had to take was admitting I didn't really understand who God was or what he thought about me.

I often feel restless. Not the kind of nomadic restlessness where I feel the urge to pack up our life, sell the house and move, more of an inability to settle down inside myself. I am known to wander around inside the house, going from room to room searching for who knows what. Purpose for the day? A project to distract myself with? A quiet place for my heart and mind to rest? Something I forgot (happening more and more) I was looking for? There's a passage of scripture in the Psalms that has always gotten my attention—especially so when that itchy restlessness is plaguing me—Be still and know that I am God (Ps 46:10). It's like the Psalmist is saying, "Here's the deal, if you don't know how to slow down, take it easy, shut your mouth and just listen...you will forever have questions about God and who He really is." Or something like that.

This idea of being still WITH God has long been a struggle for me and as I've grown in understanding myself I realize I am often plagued by "have to," "oughts," and "shoulds." This idea that if you're busy, then you're productive, and if you're productive, then you have value, you matter, you're a contributor is pervasive in our culture, families, churches and our own heads. Let me be perfectly honest, I like to matter. I like it when people notice my contribution. Sometimes too much. I also understand that I've been uniquely gifted to make a contribution and that hard work is honorable. I'm clear that "producing" isn't a bad word in and of itself and that creating and contributing has merit, worth, and value. I have been rewarded for being a "top producer," gotten attention for my offerings, and been noticed for something I've done. While I'm grateful that has been true, none of that can actually impact the place where my worth and value are established: the very heart of God.

"There isn't one more thing I can do, produce, or achieve to gain God's pleasure, love, or attention."

There isn't one more thing I can do, produce, or achieve to gain God's pleasure, love, or attention.

I didn't just magically learn how to silence the demands of the taskmaster otherwise known as the "I shoulds," so that I could be still before God. This is a discipline and like any discipline, I've had to practice it—a lot. I've practiced on my own and alongside my faith community. I've gone on retreats, read books, written pages and pages in my journal, and memorized scripture. While all that has been helpful in learning how to be still, the greatest learning has come as I've learned how to listen to what God might be trying to communicate to me during the stillness. It's one thing to be quiet, it's completely another to be attentive during the silence. To be able to simply offer myself as a ready listener as the slowing down and quieting begins, has increased my awareness that God is with me in every moment of my life and that in every one of those moments, he is also working out a very good plan for my life. This is where the learning about who God actually is has been so deeply transformative.

As I've learned to take a break from the busyness, I've begun to pay more attention and to "know" that in every sunrise, the Creator of the Universe is saying, "Welcome, here's some brand new Joy, go have a great day," and then with every setting of that same sun, there's a whisper of, "Well done, you made it. Rest now while I sing over you and we'll meet back here in the morning."

Kelly and I got married when we were basically babies (not really: 23 and 21) and bless him, I'm pretty sure if we could go back and talk to that version of my beloved husband he would tell you that he was surprised by his wife's lack of understanding of who God actually was.

As I've already shared with you, when the husband and I had been married barely a year, we decided we would start trying to get pregnant. We knew there was a chance it might be difficult and so we thought we better get going. Six years later, no baby in sight and I was a disaster. Not just physically (it felt more like a lab experiment than anything resembling romance or intimacy) but also emotionally and spiritually. Like millions before me and since, I just could not comprehend why, if God was such a good God, He wouldn't give me what I wanted? In this case, a baby. In fact, I have a very clear memory of sitting in the driveway of the very first house we owned sobbing as I communicated that very thought of God's seemingly capricious nature to my seminary attending, associate pastor husband. When I got done with my rant, that dear man took my hand, turned slightly in his seat, looked me straight in the eye and said, "You know that's not how it works, right?" In that moment, it became very clear that I did NOT know that was NOT how it worked. I had come out of my childhood with some kind of wobbly belief that if you follow the rules and make the authority figures in your life happy—you could pretty much get what you want.

That driveway conversation would be the beginning of what

I think of as my awakening. I confessed to Kelly and some trusted friends that I had very little understanding of God and His ways and would need their help and accountability as I began the journey of laying down what I thought was true about Him and discovering what was actually true.

As I "woke up," I realized that for most of my life, what I thought was true, based on the situation, was that God was either a kind Grandpa who spoiled His offspring, or He was a punishing officer of the law, ready to hand out judgment. Sometimes, like with my Cancer and my infertility, He felt both loving and punitive. As in, "Your life has been spared, but now you won't be able to have babies,"—which was incredibly confusing.

So, in this ongoing process of discovery, the most transformative truth I started encountering about God and what He's actually like is that God loves me. Beyond anything I could ever imagine, God loves me. He loves me for me. Not for anything I've done for Him or because of a certain way I look or behave or believe. This may seem basic to some, but for me this understanding of God's love was all tangled up in my productivity and busyness and achievements. I had been approaching God's love like it was a chore chart. If I memorized enough scripture, served enough people, wrote a great sermon, gave enough money, went on the mission trip...I got a gold star. Accumulate enough stars (who decides how much is "enough,") and God will pour His blessing out on me and my life.

I was in my 30s, but who cares? Is it ever too late (or too early) to learn that God is loving and kind and just and good? And, because of that goodness, He is only able to give His children gifts that are for their good?

When I was 45, I was preparing to go into the hospital for my fifth Cancer related surgery. All the tests they knew to do were inconclusive about whether the mass taking up some serious real estate on my pancreas was Cancer or not. So, the only thing left was that surgery I told you about earlier. The one with its own name, the Whipple (I've heard that if you watch Grey's Anatomy, you are familiar with this procedure). Everything I read or was told was that it was going to be a long surgery (eight - ten hours). In fact, the statistics at the time indicated that 15% of the time, people didn't survive the surgery (that number has decreased to 3% in the decade since my surgery) and beyond that, only 25% of folks who underwent the surgery survived longer than five years. With all that in mind, in the weeks leading up to the surgery, I wrote four letters. One for Kelly and then one more each for the 17, 15, and 11 year old humans I loved most in the world. I sealed those letters in an envelope, wrote "Just in Case" on the outside, and put it in a drawer under my socks and underwear.

In those letters, I tried to communicate a lot of things. Some were practical, like car payments, "do your homework," and the important account numbers. Other things were more heartfelt, like "don't forget to tell the kids you think they're amazing," begging all three kids to trust each other and their dad, and pleading with the girls to stop fighting all the time. All of it I tried to communicate without sounding frantic or afraid to die—because I wasn't. Truly, I wasn't.

There was only one thing I really wanted to say to each of them, "If this surgery takes my life, it is because God allowed it and if God allowed it, it is because there will be good in it." I wasn't talking about the kind of "good" that gives us all a warm fuzzy feeling. Rather, the kind of good we can't explain or understand in the moment (or maybe even years to come), but it is still good. I was able to say that, because the learning that got started in the driveway 18 years prior, had born life-changing fruit. I now believed with every fiber of my being that: God is good and He has and will always love you more than you could ever ask or imagine—even if you don't understand it or believe it, His goodness is still true.

I hadn't thought about those letters in a long time. As we were packing to move in with my Dad after Mom died, I found them, still hiding under my socks, in that same sealed envelope. Knowing Kelly did not have to go searching for that envelope, or hand them to our children in the backwash of my death on an operating table, still fills my heart with the kind of joy and gratitude that causes me to weep (I'm doing that now as I write these words). I'm so deeply aware that our little tribe of five is not special in the way the world views "special," we are just God's. He didn't spare my life that day because we have more faith than anyone else or were getting preferential treatment. However, what if He hadn't decided to let me live to see and experience the days that would lie ahead of me? I have so many people in my life whose story with chronic illness doesn't turn out like mine. I believe God spared my life that day and in all the days since, because He's good and the sparing has been His plan for me. If He had stopped my beating heart that day, I'm deeply convinced that this would have been a part of His goodness as well (although, let's be honest that's a part of God we will never understand).

Here's part of what I wrote to my beloved husband in his letter. I'm deeply aware I was only able to write these words down, because God and I had been sorting something big out in me, since the day Kelly gently challenged me that maybe I didn't really know "how it all works."

> We haven't been perfect and I know that. But it has been in our imperfections that the real us, the part that had to DIE has been revealed. And when we've let Him—God has done His work in and through us. For that, I will always be grateful.
>
> There's no way I can capture the last 27 years here—too much joy, sorrow, love, confusion, answers, brokenness, healing, plenty, want, laughter, anger, rejoicing, and just plain silliness. But know that every moment with you has been for my good. I'm so sorry for all the times I was being a jerk and not talking to you or ignoring you, or I was just downright mean. I love you for loving me—no matter what.
>
> And if God decides that 27 years was our time together here on earth, that is for our good as well—even though it will feel anything but "good."

I still don't know why hopeful, faithful people often don't get the things they're begging God for. A job, a life partner, the return of someone they love who walked away, a baby, shelter, restoration of their mental health, a healing. Those decisions are not mine to understand, but they are OK to question. A beloved mentor told me once, "Suze, there isn't a question you can ask God that He's not ready to handle. You can yell and scream and pound your fist about it and He's OK with that. Ask your questions." So, I have sent thousands of questions God's way and the answers don't always come back in the way I think they should or hope they will. Sometimes though, they do. What has remained steadfast and true in all my questioning, is my understanding of God's great love and goodness. Which is only possible because I decided, a long time ago sitting in a driveway with a heart full of hurt and a head full of confusion, that I didn't know everything there was to know about God and the only way to sort some of it out was to get better at the whole "be still and know..." thing.

TO CONSIDER

What lie have I believed about God and His character?

What truth could replace this lie?

What will knowing this truth change about the way I'm living?

Because change isn't a solo undertaking, who, among my trusted friends can I tell about this discovery?

EXHIBIT B: RULES? WHAT RULES?

Like all teenagers I've come in contact with, when I turned 14 or 15 I started dreaming about the freedom that would come with having my driver's license. To be able to jump in the car and launch on a great adventure any time I wanted—or at the very least run into town and get a burrito at Taco Bell—seemed like the pinnacle of independence and maturity. At the time, in Indiana, to get a driver's license you had to complete a driver's education course and complete a certain amount of hours driving a car under the supervision of an instructor. The car you practiced in could either be real (which is what I did) or a simulator (which is what my husband did and it explains a lot about his video game driving techniques). Then, when you were 16 years old, and one day (I have no idea who thought an additional day would get you any more prepared to get behind the wheel of a 1.5 ton machine?) you could take the test to get your driver's license. That was all set-up and scheduled for me to begin the summer of my 15th year. However, before I ever took a class, or got on the road with Mr. Potter (not Harry, my driver's ed teacher), or passed that exam, I was driving a car. Sneakily and illegally, I might add. I was 14 years old and my brother had the coolest car going, a burgundy El Camino, and it was parked in our driveway while he was away on a trip. It was just too tempting, and plus my mom was out running errands somewhere, and so I grabbed the keys and took it for a spin. I'm pretty sure I ended up at the little grocery store up the street from our house and made an extravagant purchase of Bubblicious bubble gum and then I drove her back home and parked it back in the driveway—no one was the wiser. I did this a couple more times, feeling more and more confident and independent every time, until about the fourth time, when I was getting out of the car to go into the grocery store and my best friend's mom Shirley (also my Mother's close friend) was coming out. She took one look at me stepping out of that El Camino and in her very uniquely Mrs. Yoder way, she loudly declared, "Susie Robbins, what are you doing? You don't have a driver's license." Busted. I believe there was some conversation about me going straight home and telling my mother or she would, and then with my stomach in my throat and my heart racing, I carefully drove the car back home and parked it for good.

Rules are important. Whether they come in the form of laws (as in, wait until you can legally drive to get behind the wheel), covenants we sign and agree to abide by, guidelines put in place to direct us along the way, or promises we make to someone we care deeply about—it matters that we have boundaries set up in our lives to keep us safe and help us stay on course.

All that said, I've never really liked what I perceived as the rigidity of rules. The rules I grew up with often felt limiting and confining, there were a lot of "have tos," "oughts," and "shoulds" in my childhood. I remember always having a bit of an achey longing inside of me for whatever might be on the other side of all those mandates. Mind you, I know now that those regulations were put in place by people in authority (parents, church leaders, teachers, coaches, etc.) who were just doing their best. Some of those folks loved me profoundly and were invested in my well-being and wanted to keep me safe. When I think about all those directives, I have gratitude for the intent behind them, AND an awareness that I grew up feeling like there was substantially more trust in the rules themselves than in me and my ability to discern the appropriateness of those guidelines. After all, two things can be true.

When my mom told me to not wander off in a department store because she may not be able to find me, there was no hiding in the clothing rack for me, I was glued to her side. When my shop teacher, Mr. Stuckey told me to wear safety goggles when I used the circular saw or a wood chip might fly up and blind me, you can bet I wore those goggles from the minute I walked into the workshop until I left. When all the Moms told us we couldn't get back in the water until an hour had passed after we ate our hotdog and chips from the snack stand or we would get a cramp, I was for sure the one sitting on the side of the pool counting down the minutes. So, when my parents told me I couldn't date until I was 16, I accepted it as a guideline my folks were putting in place for my safety. They had done the same with my siblings and I didn't question it. But when my folks came to visit me in college and my dad carefully, but firmly encouraged me to not date a young black man I was interested in because of how society might treat our imaginary future children, it felt like the guideline was carrying more weight than me and my judgment and feelings about the situation. As I matured, I found myself restless inside the boundaries for behavior that had been set up for me, and I wasn't quite sure what to do with all those unsettled feelings. What would happen if I started pulling on the threads of the cocoon of fabric these rules had created for me? Would it all unravel or would it reveal something truer to who I really was and how I wanted to live in the world?

I wouldn't know the answer to that until years later, because until I was in my mid-thirties, I followed all the rules (as best I could) and participated in no big rebellion. I did, however, secretly date that young black man in my freshman year of college. His name was Evans, and we went out a few times before and we mutually decided the relationship wasn't what either of us needed at the time.

I do believe the place I have felt the constriction of the "rules" the most is in my faith. Parental guidelines around dating and drinking and curfew-ing were normal, even if I didn't like them all the time. In the hardest of those seasons, I knew time was marching forward and I would outgrow some of those rules and they would soon be a memory. My faith though, it was going with me wherever I went, no matter what my age was or where I lived or who was paying the bills.

Did God actually care if I went to church each and every Sunday? Because that was a hard and fast rule at our house, only "broken" if we were on vacation or if I woke up vomiting.

Would I actually put my faith in jeopardy if I drank a beer or smoked a cigarette? This was a topic not even up for discussion with my folks, even though I tried many times,

Was I remaining a virgin because that is what would please God or because I was deathly afraid of my mother's wrath? I'm pretty sure the answer is the latter, even though I'd love to be able to tell you otherwise.

Were people who raised their hands in worship really just

drawing attention to themselves? Worship was a very corporate endeavor in my growing-up narrative. A personal or public expression of what was happening internally was viewed as disingenuous and attention seeking.

Was I actually failing God if I didn't give the church exactly 10% of my income? This was a hard one for me as I never really understood the "why" behind tithing, other than "that's how the pastor gets paid."

These ways of thinking, and so many more, were the rules that provided guidance to me on my emerging faith journey. It's taken me a bit of time and a lot of work to untangle some of what I believed about God and the meaning behind His genuine instructions concerning how I should live my life. There were moments of great clarity about what I believed, God as kind and benevolent and just, and then there were moments where I questioned everything. If God didn't really care that much about my church attendance, why did we talk about it so much? If God was generous, why were so many people starving and lonely and without a home? Was my sexual purity actually something God was spending a lot of time on in the Bible? If God actually had the whole world in his hands, why was this place such a disaster? If God had a good plan for my life, why did it feel that we were 100 miles away from each other and I was out here all alone? Was Mary actually a virgin? Did Lazarus actually walk out of that tomb? Was Jesus' tomb actually empty?

The time of questioning that lasted the longest was while I was in grad school. I was a pastor's wife and the mother of three young children who had been a Christian since I was 12, and yet, due to some things one of my beloved professors (who was, by the way a Jewish Agnostic) was sharing in the classroom about communities and how they should care for their citizens, I began to look deeply into what I believed and why. This season that began with some benign questions quickly turned into what I would call a crisis of faith, which lasted longer than I would have anticipated but ended up being the exact right amount of time. It began by lying in bed every night, trying to fall asleep while my brain was buzzing with doubt and skepticism. I would lie there for hours it seemed wrestling with the question of

God's reality and His goodness. After a couple of weeks I was tired of the questioning. It didn't seem like I was gaining any clarity. Instead, now I was sleep deprived and I still had all my questions. I began to wonder, during the daytime now, about proof, facts, and evidence. Had I just blindly believed what I was told in Vacation Bible School and Sunday School and at the supper table? I called my pastor husband and informed him I was quitting. "Quitting what?," was his reply. "My faith," I said, "It just doesn't make any sense to me anymore." Silence on his end and then, "I'll be right home." After hearing me out, Kelly gave me an assignment. He told me to take some 3x5 cards and write out everything I believed (or thought I believed) about God and then, when I felt like I had exhausted my list, spread it all out on the dining room table and just read them, sit with them, don't make any judgment about them. Then, after I had read them through a few times, decide what I do/do not believe and pick those cards up and throw the rest out.

That task, given to me I'm sure with love and a bit of panic, changed my life. I was 34-years-old and it was the first time I had taken the time to really examine and think about what I believed and what I didn't. Not what my parents or friends or pastor husband believed, but what I was actually being held in my head and close to my heart.

I covered that table with 3x5 cards. I walked past them for days. I read through them at least five times. Then I made two piles, one for what I didn't actually believe or was ambivalent about, and a pile for what I did believe. I can't tell you all the things that were in the discarded pile, but I can tell you the five things I held onto:

1. God is omnipotent, omniscient and omnipresent.
2. God is the Creator of the world.
3. God is loving and good and just—this happens by being Three.
4. Jesus is who he said he was, and did the things people say he did and is still doing them.
5. I am fearfully and wonderfully made and there's a good plan being worked out in my life.

I'm 57 now and these five things have held fast for me. They have become the "rules," if you will, for my life and allowed me to not get so tangled up in whatever might be the religious or political controversy of the season. It's not that I'm not aware of or ignoring topics or ideas that seem to be stirring things up in the church (which by the way is not new) or the culture around the church. Rather, my understanding that God is an all loving, creative, good and just God, that the Holy Spirit has my back, that Jesus is the Son of God and is the antithesis of, and answer for, everything that's wrong in the world, and that I am living out a really good plan for my life all while having been created in the image of the Divine allows me to know my place and find my voice, rather than have to be right about all the things.

What I'm saying is I don't have to have all the answers and know exactly what I think, forever and always, about women in ministry, inclusion, healing the sick, racial reconciliation, the Church's response to mental illness, abortion, marriage after divorce, politics, and all the other things—because God is God and hallelujah, I'm not. It has been the times (and trust me there have been plenty) that I have forgotten what I know to be true about God, that my faith has gotten wobbly and I have wavered in my understanding of my place in the world. Do I have to know exactly what I think and what the theological framework is on sexual identity in order for me to love my neighbor who identifies as gay? Is it imperative that I have everything sorted out so I can clearly articulate my theology on healing for me to believe and pray that God will (and can) heal my friend of her mental illness? Must I be able to convince the men of the church, by providing a thorough and exhaustive study of the scriptures, that scripture means it when it says there is no difference between the Jew or the Gentile, the slave or the free, and the male and female—because as far as it matters, we are are all one in Christ (Galatians 3:28)?

In Chapters Five, Six, and Seven of his retelling of his time with Jesus, Matthew (one of the disciples) covers a lot of territory, telling us what he observed and heard Jesus talking about when it came to anger and murder, lust and adultery, divorce and remarriage, loving our enemies, taking care of those who have need, prayer, worry, and asking God for the things we long for. Overarchingly, for me, these three chapters are a reminder that Jesus came not to wipe out all the rules the Jewish people were living by (there were 365 by the way), but rather to be the fully alive example of "how to live a Godly life." All those rules, and all ours too, are complete and fulfilled in the person of Jesus—not in a handbook or a denomination's doctrinal statement.

As a fellow human, I get our on again, off again love affair with rules and guidelines like speed limits and bedtimes and the 10 items or less line at the grocery store. They provide boundaries and instruction for us, until they don't. Roads wind in and out of cities and towns and stretches of highway, so the speed limit changes. Kids grow and mature, hopefully, and so bedtimes change and grow with them. And the 10 item or less lane? That seems more like a suggestion than a rule.

"I don't have to have all the answers and know exactly what I think, forever and always, about women in ministry, inclusion, healing the sick, racial reconciliation, the Church's response to mental illness, abortion, marriage after divorce, politics, and all the other things—because God is God and hallelujah, I'm not."

When it comes to our faith, the same can be true. What was meant to serve as wise counsel for a life of faith, like treating your body as a temple, turned into unyielding evidence of a person's holiness or lack thereof.

When our kids were young, we would sometimes go bowling. It was one of those activities I never thought to do when the kids were bored or it was a rainy summer day and then when we would go, and have a blast, I would think, "Why don't we do this more often?" Before the offspring were strong enough to do more than a two handed, between the legs, "who knows where this ball is going to land," toss down the lane, we would put the bumpers up. Bowling bumpers are those magical guides that kept the ball inside the lane, even if it was going so slowly you could count the rotations. Eventually you gain a certain proficiency in the game and you don't need the bumpers anymore (but I think this is a rumor made up by better bowlers because I personally still need those bumpers every now and then).

In my faith life, my "bumpers" were the rules I lived by and they have been found through lots of different people and things: my parents, church, my christian college experience, my seminary trained husband, the pastor, a favorite author, and rarely myself.

Early on, they provided the kind of help I needed to keep headed in the right direction, but eventually I had to learn how to love and serve and repent and pray and trust and believe and change my mind and about things and trust myself—based on what God says and not what the "bumpers" were saying or doing.

I've spent some time thinking about how to discern what's "right" or "wrong" and I wonder if maybe we've made all this rule keeping and following more complicated than it was ever meant to be. What if the guidelines, put in place to help us, have turned into the very things that are holding us back from the life God intended for us? For instance, what if God doesn't really care that much if I'm in church every Sunday of the year, but rather cares deeply about the fact that I have a true, honest, vibrant community of faith-filled people in my life?

Years ago, I had a friend who was trying to help me get untangled from a bit of a mess that had emerged in my life from my efforts to please anyone and everyone. Mostly I did this by trying to "get it all right" (aka: follow the rules). She shared with me the best (and maybe only?) questions I needed to ask on a daily basis and I've been practicing asking those questions for nearly a decade and it's changed a lot about how I respond to someone or what I do when I feel stuck on what is next:

1. God, what are you saying?
2. God, what should I do about what you're saying?

Asking these questions has radically changed the way I follow

Jesus. This discipline, because that's what it is, has taught me to understand that not only does God have a thought about every single aspect of my life, He wants to help me rely on the three of Him for the navigation of that life, rather than a set of rules.

TO CONSIDER

What lie have I believed about God and the rules He has given us to live by?

What truth could replace this lie?

What will knowing this truth change about the way I'm living?

Because change isn't a solo undertaking, who, among my trusted friends can I tell about this discovery?

EXHIBIT C: THAT BUTTERFLY THING

Transformation. Change. Modification. Variation. Amendment. Metamorphosis. Evolution. Whatever word you use for it, I'm convinced we're all invited to go on a journey to becoming better humans. If we choose to go on it, like every journey I've ever been on, there's a beautiful and painful part to the adventure.

I've long been fascinated by the moves a caterpillar must make to become a butterfly. To begin as a brown, squishy crawling bug and wind up a flying thing of beauty and grace has always blown my mind. When our kids were in third grade, their teacher Mrs. Hewett (the best teacher of all time ever) included a butterfly unit in her curriculum. The kids were to gather milkweed plants, Mrs. H. provided the larva, and then the kiddos would do the work of feeding, watching, and waiting. When it was time, the class would invite the parents in for the big release party. We went through this three times; each of the kids had Mrs. H., and each time I remember the frustration of having to wait for that butterfly to hatch. Usually it took about two weeks, and each day after school the butterfly report would be "not today," until the day when the hatching happened. Waiting for transformation is like that. Long, frequently frustrating, mostly tedious, and sometimes boring. We've been told, or we're hoping with everything we've got, that change is coming. There has been a promise of something beautiful at the end of the waiting and yet—it feels like that day will never come, until it does. And just like that, the transformation is real.

I'm convinced we get trained on this longing for change at an early age. As babies, many of us get fed and held and begin to settle into a sweet slumber, and then some larger person has the audacity to lay us down. If we had verbal skills at that moment, I'm convinced we would say something like, "I do not like this current situation, please do something to make it better." There's a longing for something more, something different, or "other" that I think gets sparked into life then and for many, lasts a very long time. Left unattended, this longing can turn into discontent quickly, at least it did for me.

Over the years, I've changed a lot. I have gained and lost the same 50 pounds three times (thank you Weight Watchers). My hair has gone from deep brown to a silvery gray and my once unlined face now has lots of "smile lines." My body was born with several parts that I no longer hold inside my frame and I've had to learn to live without them. We've moved 10 times in 35 years of marriage and I've held 14 different jobs in 12 different organizations in that same time frame. I've gone from being single, to married, to childless, to the mother of three. Our home was full and loud and chaotic, and had all that comes with having three children, and then it wasn't because they grew up and headed out on their own. I have been someone's daughter and then my parents both died and I was no one's child. I used to think I knew exactly what I thought and felt about big things like race and gender equality, response to trauma, and inclusion, and now I'm weighing and sorting some of those thoughts, because I'm not sure I believe what I used to believe.

Yet, even with all this change, for a long time my heart kept aching for more, better, different. There was something way down inside me that could not, would not, be satisfied no matter what modifications I was making in my life. Come to find out, it wasn't about what the scale said or the color of my hair or the context for my work. What I didn't yet understand was the mystery of how transformation actually happens. In this season I often felt like I was looking at one of those 3D paintings that had a picture hidden inside the picture—I just couldn't see it. As I've shared in an earlier chapter, part of the clarity I needed would come from learning more about who God truly was. The other part would come as I learned how to hear His voice amidst all the noise, like kids and work and culture and bills getting paid, in my life. I also knew that what needed to be different inside me needed to be transformed, not just modified. Like a badly installed electrical socket that keeps burning out every lightbulb you put in it, I needed to be rewired from the inside out.

As a person of faith, I knew where this transformation would come from. This kind of radical change was the very thing Jesus told his believers he came for. To take the things inside you, the way you think, act, and believe, and change them to reflect the way Jesus himself thought, acted, and believed.

I spent a lot of time in my early adult years wanting to change. Whether it was my work life, my spiritual life, or in my relational world, I would find myself longing for something that seemed just out of reach. In all areas of my life, I wanted to have more faith, to trust God more deeply, to be generous to a fault, to live in the mystery that comes with following God, to rejoice authentically in my suffering. Over and over I wrote about all of this in my journal and I complained to my friends that something needed to be "better" or "more" than it was. I would commit to start practicing living life like that and then something would happen—our bank account would start to run short, my health would take a turn for the not great, I would have more questions about parenting than I would have answers—and it would send me running back to living by sight, not by faith. I started calling this pattern the "great cycle of lament."

I've been working on a theory for a while now as to why my thinking and beliefs kept tripping me up. I think I was a little like the followers of Jesus when he was teaching them about what would be required to follow him. He tells them it will be necessary for some of them to risk their very lives. As soon as that came out of his mouth, many of them responded with, "This teaching is too hard," and walked away. They believed Jesus might be who he said he was, and most likely wanted to live the life he was calling them to, but when it came down to it they didn't have enough faith in the wholeness of who Christ was and what he could do to change what they believed and how they lived. For me, that seemed to be at the crux of my unwillingness to change—I believed Jesus was who he said he was, but did I believe in him enough to pay the price required to follow him into the life he was inviting me to?

As a teenager with a potentially terminal illness, I wrestled with a very real fear of dying. I also had a lot of other fears. I was worried about my spot on the track and tennis teams, my role in the spring musical, if I would be able to take driver's education, where would I stand with my friends when it was all said and done, and what about my hair—was it going to betray me and fall out? These were all marked as losses, real or potential, and I grieved them as only a scared teenage girl would, which meant I did my share of pouting and crying and getting a tiny bit grumpy.

For the diagnosis and treatment phases of my journey, I was hospitalized in one of only a couple children's hospitals in Indiana and it was a couple hours from home. Mom carried the buik of the caregiving load, spending days and weeks away from home. Every now and then, to give her a break, my completely gray and wrinkly grandparents would get in their 14-year-old car and make a three hour drive to sit by my bed, see my face, hold my hand, and work on a crossword puzzle. On one of those visits, I remember being particularly disappointed about something I had "lost" (I think my spot in the school play) and I was throwing a bit of a fit when my grandparents walked in. I don't believe I asked "why" very often, as in "Why me?" "Why now?" But this time I was not just asking, I was demanding an answer for a question that had none.

My granddad was a man of few words; we all knew when he spoke, it was because he felt he had something important to say. On this day, this man who, in my hearing, never uttered a complaint, listened to my rant. When I say "listened," I mean he really heard me. He was listening underneath the words of my tirade and behind my tears and perceived what I was actually saying, "Would I be here next year to get to experience those things or was I experiencing the end of me?"

When I was done, this gentle, loving farmer/teacher/granddad of mine took my hand, looked me right in the eye and said, "You're going to be fine. It's all going to work out and next year will be your year." Simple words for a not so simple situation—but they were what

> *"I also knew that what needed to be different inside me needed to be transformed, not just modified. Like a badly installed electrical socket that keeps burning out every lightbulb you put in it, I needed to be rewired from the inside out."*

I needed and desperately wanted to believe. I believed in my Grand-father's love, AND I believed what it was he was telling me to do: take a breath, draw on your faith, and trust everyone around you.

That's what I mean about believing Jesus is who he says he is, but not believing IN him in such a way that I would stop resisting the change he wanted to bring to my life. For instance, I would have told you back then that I believed Jesus was the son of God, but if I had been completely transparent, I would have told you I did NOT believe he could make a way where there seemed to be no way, so I better go find a way all by myself.

Back to Gramps, this man had never lied to me in all the years that lead up to that day in the hospital—why would he have started then? So when he told me things were going to get better, that I was going to get better, and all that "better" would be for my good, I believed him and I believed in what he was telling me. You know what, Gramps was right—the next year was my year, and so was the one after that, and the one after that, and the one…you get the point.

My very wise second-born child has told me, more than once, that the only transformation that actually "sticks" is the change that comes from self-discovery—the willingness to look deep inside and address that longing for "different." Part of the reason I kept falling into the pattern of the "great cycle of lament" was that I was consistently hoping the catalyst for change would come from the outside—that someone or something else would fix whatever was wrong with me or my life. In actuality, everything I needed for the transformation to take place was inside me all along. The Bible says that transformation happens when we change our mind about something and that same verse tells me that the actual transformation is not up to me, God's the only one who can do that, but the mindset shift is my responsibility.

Makes sense to me. I too was a baby, young child, and teenager who was shaped by the unmet longing in my life. God says he has placed a piece of eternity inside every human heart (Ecc. 3:11) and because that's true, we will always experience a powerful pull toward something that forever seems just out of reach. Maybe that's the journey then—to continue to change, modify, alter, reconstruct, and sometimes even metamorphose, until that piece of eternity inside us is reunited with the whole of itself once and for all in Heaven.

To be transformed then, has very little to do with changing our circumstance, or weight, or job, or the house we live in. Instead, it has everything to do with altering all the places people may not be able to see, but are no less real. Our hearts, our minds, our way of thinking—to experience a radical reshaping of what was or is unto what might be, is the powerful and painful work of reshaping the interior of our lives.

A gentle reminder here and a difficult lesson I seem to have to keep re-learning: help will be needed for this. As a person of faith, I've had transformational assistance from a therapist, friends, family, time alone, spiritual direction, journalling, and the supernatural guidance of the Holy Spirit.

Today, I have an unwavering belief that I am different from who I used to be. I'm not perfect by any means (that's not a thing), but I am being transformed into something that more authentically reflects the goodness of God that is inside me. On my own, none of this change would or could happen. It's happening because I believe Jesus is the son of God AND I believe that when He calls me to something I don't understand or He makes a promise I desperately long for Him to keep, no matter how confused or desperate I get—clarity will come and His promises will always be kept (sometimes just not on this side of Heaven). With all that I am, I am convinced He is who He says He is and that He can do what He says he can do.

Any faith I have today, that I have all I need to navigate life in a way that doesn't leave me feeling panicky when things get difficult, is built on the foundation of all the answered prayers from all the yesterdays and tomorrows, not from believing a lie that says I can earn God's love or live a faith-filled life all on my own. I may have thought I was asking God for a job or a healing or a way out when there seemed to be none, but what He provided through his answers was transformation.

For that, I am sure I will spend the rest of my life expressing my gratitude.

TO CONSIDER

What lie have I believed about my ability to change—as in to be transformed—and my responsibility in that transformation?

What truth could replace this lie?

What will knowing this truth change about the way I'm living?

Because change isn't a solo undertaking, who, among my trusted friends can I tell about this discovery?

EXHIBIT D: SPIRITUAL CHILDREN (AND GRANDCHILDREN TOO)

I became a Christian when I was 12, or so the story goes. Truth be told, I don't have any memory of what my life was like before I made that decision or even what the catalyst was for me to make it. My mother always said 12 was the "age of accountability," so I'm sure we had a conversation about it and I prayed a prayer. Honestly, it's not a clear memory for me—which over the years has caused me some anxiety. I mean, shouldn't you be able to remember the day, the hour, the moment when you made the most important decision of your life? I don't have a "salvation anniversary" date, I have the general vicinity of sometime during the year 1977.

I was a church kid in the 60s and 70s who was being raised in all the ways church kids were raised then: go to Sunday School every Sunday, learn how to do the "basics" like praying before meals and bed, singing a hymn or two, tithing, and listening during the Sunday sermon. As a child, I went to Vacation Bible School in the summer and then when I was older, the youth group retreat in the winter. I don't remember the catalyst behind leaning over in the pew one Sunday and telling my dad I wanted to get baptized—maybe it was just the right time. I grew up in what was lovingly called the "dunkard" tradition (not to be confused with a drunkard tradition), which just meant that when you got baptized at my church, it happened by being fully immersed in a body of water. My siblings got baptized by our Uncle Art, who was a pastor, in a stream in Pennsylvania. It was cold and the stream was shallow and my brother was trying to catch fish between his knees. I wanted a story like that, but my baptism was pretty ordinary: wear modest clothing under a white robe, walk down the three steps into the tank at the front of the church, and get dunked.

Even though I came to faith as a pre-teen and got baptized pretty quickly after that, I spent a lot of nights fighting sleep in my childhood room with Pepto Bismol pink walls, convinced that I would go to hell if I tragically died in the night.

I've talked to so many folks in my generation about their faith journey. Our stories are pretty similar—many of us grew up in Christian families that rarely talked about faith with any sense of intimacy, and attended churches and youth groups where many of us either felt coerced or guilted into a decision about our faith (this was the era of the A Thief in the Night movies which basically scared the crap out of people so they would accept Christ). It seemed like the priority all along the way was to become a Christian, not necessarily to become a disciple. It would take me another 20 years to transition from just professing faith in Jesus to the kind of transformative faith that changes you in ways that you never turn away from. The kind of faith that has very little to do with how you feel in a specific moment but rather, what you know is true about God and His love for you.

Don't get me wrong, I do believe my faith was authentic and life-changing when I prayed that prayer of salvation as a kid. I'm also just as confident that there was so much more I could have known and experienced. It's not as if I didn't get wet enough in my baptism or the tomb wasn't empty enough for me to be called a believer. However, I do often wonder how my 20s and 30s would have been different if I had been invited (and accepted the invite) to lay down what I thought I knew and explore God in a way that was deeply personal and transformative. In other words, to be disciples.

For nearly three decades, I went to church faithfully, attended a Christian university, signed up for classes, studies and groups, read the chapters, filled in the blanks, and memorized the "right" answers and yet, those childhood nights of wondering if I was actually going to "make it in" stuck with me. Would God actually welcome me Home or would he stand at the door with a list of my transgressions and deny me entrance? Those are the kinds of questions, I've learned, someone without a clear understanding on who God is and how he interacts with his children asks. There was a lot of carryover from my relationship with my dominant parental figure, Mom, who kept a running list of my "mess ups" and I knew if the list grew too long, there would be consequences like getting grounded, missing events with friends, and in the early years, the occasional spanking. Consequently, I didn't have a clear understanding of the kind of grace God deals in and the impact it would have on my life.

I started reading when I was very young. I was raised in a family of readers and my folks were always asking, "does everybody have something to read?" For me, books were a bridge, between the "here" and the "someplace else"—a place I may never get to travel to, with people who, if they were real, I might fall in love with or end up loathing. Every Monday in the summer, with my library card in hand, I rode my bike to the top of the hill and climbed the three steps up into the most magical place I could imagine—the book mobile. A portable library—what could be better for a seven-year-old greedy reader? Reading was a huge part of my growing up story and I was ruthless about it. If I didn't quite "get" the plot in the first few chapters, I would skip ahead and see if it got more interesting, if it didn't, I didn't finish the book. If I cared deeply about a character and his/her journey in the plot, I've been known to read the last chapter before finishing the book to see if something horrible happens to them; if it did, I didn't finish the book. If you're recommending a book to me, the worst thing you can tell me is, "Hang in there, it starts out slow but gets better about halfway through." Nope, I'm out. I display a little more stick-to-it-ness if I have purchased the book, after all that was good money I spent and I better find a way to enjoy the book. Even then though, with money on the line—if I don't like it, I don't like it and it goes into the "sell" or "donate" pile.

Recently, as I was dropping off yet another stack of books at the "buy back" used bookstore (where I would make a whopping $4.98 for my $200 worth of books), I thought about how my approach to books is a lot like my approach to grace. There doesn't seem to be any gray area with me and books—it's either worth it, or not. The question I asked myself as I roamed the aisles of the bookstore awaiting my big payout was, "Is this how I view God's approach to me?" How many times have I been afraid that if I'm not good enough, God's going to walk away from me? What if I don't have my stuff together by "page 41," and God closes the book and that's it for me? In my rational mind, I know that's not what happens, but often, when we're afraid, it's not our rational mind talking to our heart.

Grace is favor, not asked for or deserved, freely given and I know I have received that, over and over in all the years I've been following Jesus. But what if there's a limit? That's the nagging question for me. Rationally, I know that's not true. But when I'm in the thick of something—hardship, sin, disobedience, suffering of any kind—it can sure feel like grace has a switch and any moment, it's going to get flipped to "off."

It was this kind of thinking, this way of feeling actually, that brought me to the end of myself in my mid-40s. I was the mom of three teenagers, on the pastoral team at a large church, married to a pastor at that same church, a person struggling with chronic illness, and a worn-out and weary follower of Jesus who knew there was more to learn and live by about God's provision and grace. However, I wasn't sure how to go about the learning or the living. I was struggling with crippling people-pleasing and an insatiable need for external approval and it was starting to have an impact everywhere. I had a boss who I think liked me OK, but wasn't overly supportive of my spiritual gift of teaching and the expression of it in the church. I was in the midst of one of the more difficult seasons with my Mom. I was spending a lot of energy and time trying to figure out how to make her happy so I could gain the approval from her I desperately longed for. I was worried about the kids as they entered their teenage years and the ongoing concern about finances and "would there ever be enough" thinking. All of this I held close to my vest, thinking how could I share with anyone but the husband and maybe a couple others? I was on the pastoral staff at a church after all, what would that have been like if I had admitted I wasn't really clear on grace, one of the fundamentals of our faith?

In the midst of this season, my friend Steph asked me if I would like to enter into a discipling relationship with her. This wouldn't be a Bible Study or getting together for coffee to "talk it out." This would be a year-long commitment, with her and a few other women, shaped by intention and purpose, so that I could learn to follow

Jesus, by following her example as she did the same. I had been a Christian for 30 years and in all those years I had never been invited into this kind of a relationship. I had been preaching and teaching about Jesus' invitations to "make disciples who make disciples" and yet, I hadn't been through the process myself.

That year changed my life. Six of us met once a week, for two hours in Steph's living room and then sometimes we would get together individually with her or go out into the world and serve together. There was a book we all read, concepts we learned together so we would have shared language, and homework. Always homework. More than all of that though, there was Steph's life and the way she was living it out in front of all of us. The example I was given and the truths we explored together would prove to be the beginning of my understanding of just how much I still had to learn about who God really was (and is). I would explore how far I had walked away from my true self, the version of me that God had fearfully and wonderfully made and that had gotten covered up over lots of years of doing things "for" God rather than "with" God. It would be during these twelve months that I would learn how my actual identity had nothing to do with anything I did, but rather everything to do with the words God uses to describe me (daughter, beloved, miracle, masterpiece, and free, to name a few) and how deeply and profoundly I am loved by the One who made me. It would be in understanding this kind of Love that would finally and forever teach me about the kind of grace that looks at, and then through, my flaws and only sees the reflection of the Divine that dwells in me. As I began to understand what it actually meant when Jesus invited people, over and over, to follow him—my heart longed to do just that. Not because anyone was watching or because I was getting paid to do it, but because I couldn't imagine doing anything else in my life. To have my heart and ears attuned to the voice of God and then to do something with whatever I heard Him saying to me, became the longing of my heart and the purpose of my life. I was rediscovering myself and my faith and it was exciting.

It wasn't an instantaneous change—I did, after all spend three decades listening to my own voice first, and trying to get God's plans to fit mine—but it was a transformative shift in the way I lived and still live. I don't ever want to go back to relying on myself first and God second—even though I'm tempted daily. I want to live immersed in grace, so I can then pass it on.

For me, it's that "passing it on" part that has proven to be the definer between becoming a believer and becoming a disciple. Don't get me wrong, believing is imperative. However, as a disciple I must pass along what I'm learning, how I'm changing, the ways God is moving in my life. I'm called to make disciples who make disciples who make disciples who make disciples... I was the spiritual daughter of my friend who invested a year of her life into mine. I wanted to give her some spiritual grandchildren.

So, over the years I have invited some friends, just like I had been invited, to follow me as I followed Jesus. Not perfectly (because that is NOT a thing), but in a real and lively way. We would learn together what it means to listen to God and do what He says—sometimes that was as easy as breathing and often it came at great risk to the listener. These women took what they knew about God and their relationship with Him and explored if it could be more. It can always be more. That's as simple and complex an answer as I know to, "Is there more to learn?" I will spend the rest of my life learning what it means to be God's daughter and His Good News ambassador.

The first "friends" I invited (although not formally) were my children. After all, if I wasn't living a life worth imitating with my own children and they were not being invited to become disciples, what did it matter if I was doing that with other people's sons and daughters? To be honest, it was kind of a hit or miss endeavor, for a variety of reasons. We had already spent lots of years together; all three of them were believers, and each was on his/her own journey of shaping their faith. I decided though, if we could just practice listening to God together and then being obedient, that would be an investment worth making. We talked about three basic concepts together and they were modeled after the directional way Jesus built relationships: UP with God the Father, IN with other believers, and OUT into the hurting world. Where were we spending most of our time? As a family we decided it was UP and IN which revealed a huge gap in our family's pursuit of OUT. We began to look for ways to have conversations with non-believing people in our world and the kids themselves identified that they had a great OUT opportunity as they all attended public school.

For the majority of this season, Mackenzie was the only one left at home. As the youngest, she was witness to some of her parent's greatest transformation, whether she recognized it as such or not. The summer before her junior year in High School, she began to have some anxiety. School was hard, she shared with us, and one of the things that made it really difficult was that often, she would be the only Christian—at the lunch table, in the cast for the play, or part of the study group. We talked a lot that summer about what we should do. Should she stay where she was or should we apply for the Christian high school down the road from our house? But more than talk, we decided to practice UP, IN, and OUT for a specific timeframe, specifically asking God for an answer to this

"As I began to understand what it actually meant when Jesus invited people, over and over, to follow him—my heart longed to do just that. Not because anyone was watching or because I was getting paid to do it, but because I couldn't imagine doing anything else in my life."

question of where Mackenzie should go to school. The three of us spent time with God in prayer together, asking Him what Mackenzie should do. All three of us talked with other believers and invited them to pray with us. We spent time OUT, with friends who weren't believers and serving in our community that we deeply love. At the end of time we had set aside, Mackenzie felt like she was supposed to stay put and so did we. We did keep practicing UP, IN, and OUT and I do believe it changed the trajectory of that year for her.

I'm not a huge believer in regret, I think it's kind of a cop-out because as long as I'm breathing, I can do what I can to make a wrong situation right. So I don't regret not inviting the kids earlier into a more intentional disciple-making relationship, I just wish the language we share today would've been true when they were younger.

Here's what I've learned, God sometimes answers prayers we forgot we prayed. Before we ever had children, Kelly and I asked God to give us what we needed to be our future offsprings' first "pastors," not because this is what we did for a living, but because we wanted our children to learn about Jesus from us. As the kids were growing up, God gave us what we needed, when we needed it, and even when we ignored what He was offering. When I look back, it's clear to me that God made a way for our kids to know Him, no matter what my husband and I were or were not doing. Were we perfect at parenting in the way of Jesus? I'm not even sure what that means, but probably not. Here's what I do know: our kids watched too much TV, had cell phones earlier than was necessary, went to PG13 movies way before they turned thirteen, hung out with people who hurt their feelings, were treated unjustly, and they themselves were unfair in their treatment of others. Our three were "out there," mixing it up with a culture that didn't (and still doesn't for that matter) care for them or even really like them. Our children, as all children have, were wounded by a world of comparison and competition that is no respecter of age or experience. There was also plenty of joy and celebration with those three first disciples. Imagining, hoping, and dreaming God sized dreams were part of their growing up as well. I'm convinced it's all of these things, the wins and the losses, that do the real shaping of us as we grow and mature. Today, each of the three has a deep and abiding faith and it's their own. Not mine. Not their Dad's. It's personal and real and true and each, in their own ways, have taught (and will keep teaching) others to follow Jesus as they follow him.

As I've shared earlier, in my mid-40s, I was going through a particularly tough time with my Mom. I remember stopping over at Mom and Dad's house (we just lived 15 minutes from each other) one afternoon and when I got there she was napping. I went back and she was just waking up and patted the spot next to her on the bed. It was such a sweet, intimate olive branch moment, I will never forget it. As we lay there, both looking up at the ceiling, I gathered up my courage and asked her a question I had been longing to ask her since my ongoing misunderstanding of grace had become increasingly more of a challenge in my own growth and development. "Mom, how come we never really talked about Grace when I was growing up?" After a long pause, without excuse or energy, she just gently replied, "Oh honey, I never knew enough about it to tell you anything worthwhile."

I've thought about that moment on the bed with my mom often. Lots of things started to make sense as I lay beside her in the silence that followed her confession. Mostly, we only want to talk with other people about the things we've become expert in. Because at the core of our need for grace is some kind of failure or deficit, we won't ever feel like an expert in it and consequently, we find ourselves not talking about grace very much.

After that talk with Mom, I began awakening to the overwhelming truth that without both an understanding of, and experience with, grace and mercy, becoming a true disciple of Christ will always be just out of reach. I can know about him, and his power and provision and judgment, but if I'm not clear that he will forever offer me a particular kind of clemency that I could never earn on my own, it will all just be an idea or theory. God is always and forever inviting us into a more intimate relationship with Him and that relationship is where grace lives.

I left lots of hurt and frustration on the bed that day with my mom and as we got up and moved back into the day, I took with me a resolve that I hold to this day: I will know and experience God in ways that bring Him honor and others blessing. I will also seek out others to help me on that journey. As well, I will be faithful to tell anybody who wants to know more about grace or faith or forgiveness or joy, or how to live the kind of life Jesus invites us all to.

TO CONSIDER

What lie have I believed about my ability to become a true disciple and my responsibility to disciple others?

What truth could replace this lie?

What will knowing this truth change about the way I'm living?

Because change isn't a solo undertaking, who, among my trusted friends can I tell about this discovery?

PART 3: RELATIONSHIPS

LIE

Something in me is fundamentally wrong, and I can't have healthy, functional relationships.

TRUTH

Relationships are complicated and yet key to thriving, robust living. No one has this figured out and so, the adventure is in the practice of building relationships, not in mastering a skill.

For as long as I can remember, I have felt like I was somehow missing the mark in my relational world. As a kid, I longed for intimacy with my mother, as a teenager I wanted friendships with bonds that couldn't be broken, as a young married woman I wanted to understand my husband and I wanted him to understand me, and, in my 30s and 40s, making new friends felt like a locked safe I could not crack. For years, I kept spinning the dial trying to get access to something everyone else seemed to have already figured out. What I know now is that everyone is just doing their best when it comes to relationships. Moment by moment, interaction by interaction, folks are just trying, and they keep trying, hoping to get it right more times than they get it wrong.

Belonging has long been my kryptonite. In every place and every circle (except the one that holds who I'm married to and the three I raised), I find myself asking, "Do I belong here?" And the follow-up question is often, "What do I need to do, and who do I need to be, so I can belong here?" Over the years, I've had to sort through the frequently self-manufactured complicatedness that often feels true in my relationships. With my parents, my husband, and in my friendships, the ongoing choices I've been faced with are to pick community or stay isolated, and to repair or ignore the harm I've caused because of a miscommunication.

These days, health in my relational world is happening in places and with people where I can be Suze. The real me. I don't need to perform or be funny or dazzle with cleverness. Instead, you and I can both be curious about each other, give each other the kind of grace we are individually receiving from the Father, and trust each other's heart for the other. I think relationships are a marathon and I've nearly thrown in the towel many times but the way my heart feels when that deep connection with another happens is like a cup of cold water in mile 17 and the race is back on. (I have never, ever in my life, run a marathon, but you know what I mean.)

The evidence I present in the following chapters is to confront the lie that relationships are easy and don't take a lot of work. Healthy relationships are worth fighting for—even when they are complicated or confusing, and a big part of that "fight" is found in the knowledge I hold in my own identity and what I'm offering, both helpful and hurtful, to the people in my relational world.

Love is what carries you, for it is always there,
even in the dark, or most in the dark,
but shining out at times like gold stitches
in a piece of embroidery.

—WENDELL BERRY[1]

Exhibit A: Children Should Be Seen And Not Heard

I am the mother of three pretty spectacular children. Two of them are female. I was, and sometimes still am, terrified to be their mother (of the boy child, too, but that's a story for another time). None of that terror is or ever was founded in anything that had to do with the girls. They were both easy babies, super healthy and happy, and they slept like champs from the time they were five weeks old. They have grown into young women who have a particular kind of ease around them—pretty typical twenty-somethings who are joyful, funny, worried about the things I cannot talk them out of worrying about, and deeply connected to their faith.

Nope, my fear of mothering these two girls was rooted in my own relationship with my own mom and the places in my heart where, as a girl, I wish she and I would have done better. As I've shared earlier, my mom was a rule-maker and a rule-keeper, and I was a child who chafed at the rules. I have words now to say that those rules felt like they were creating a barrier between her and me, a chasm that, by the time I was in my late twenties, made her feel unreachable. I also know now that my mother had a fiercely protective nature and any rule she established was, for her, a way to keep me safe in a world she saw as incredibly broken and dangerous. I didn't know all that as a child, but I did know that the safest place in the world was in her arms, yet I have very few memories of being held there. I understand now that my mother was fighting for my life, but back then it just felt like she was fighting me.

By the time my parents found out they were expecting me, my mom was years deep into an unresolved grief around her own mother's death and that lack of resolution would have a big impact on me and our relationship together.

Mom was the youngest of five children, raised by Israel and Esther Royer. Just let those names sink in a minute. She was raised both in town and on the farm in eastern Pennsylvania. From every story I've ever heard, my mother's mother was a force to be reckoned with. The daughter of a self-made millionaire, my grandmother was, at 6'2" and over 230lbs, both figuratively and literally, a giant in people's lives—especially my Mom's. When my mom left Pennsylvania to attend college in Indiana, leaving her mother was the hardest of goodbyes.

In Indiana, mom met dad at Manchester College where they were Biology lab partners. She was fulfilling a general education requirement and he was sorting out that he did NOT want to be a doctor. According to both of them, it was love at first sight. He just had to go home and break up with his girlfriend before mom would say yes to a date. She had rules, even back then.

My parents got engaged within four months of meeting each other and married just a few months after that. My dad started coaching high school basketball and teaching algebra, and my sister was soon on her way. By the time my mom was expecting my brother, my folks had moved a few times. Dad was still coaching and teaching, and mom was at home with soon-to-be two kiddos under three, and my brother had the audacity to be due during my dad's basketball season. So, as women often do when there are gaps in the keeping-it-all-running front, my mom called her mom to come help with my sister while she was in the hospital with the baby. As they were driving west, my grandfather at the wheel, hurtling down the turnpike to get my grandmother to Indiana to be with my mom, my grandmother turned and reached into the back seat for a salty, Pennsylvania hard pretzel and had a massive coronary in the car. My grandmother never made it past the Ohio state line. My mother's giant had fallen and honestly, looking back, I think a big part of my mom never recovered.

Fast forward five years, and my folks find out I am going to make them a family of five. I was a "surprise" as they say in the "how to tell your unexpected child you weren't really planning on her without saying she was an accident" manual. Where my sister had been eager to please and my brother had been quiet and cooperative as a baby, I was loud and demanding. My father used to tell me I had always been full of "piss and vinegar," which I never really understood but always acknowledged as being somewhat unpleasant.

I was loved, there was no doubt in my mind about that. However, I was also, as you remember, not something or someone they had planned on, and as I've said, our house was set to run by Mom's rules and I was not the most proficient at keeping those rules. Some of the rules were actually the guidelines most parents put in place in an effort to raise children who don't run wild, eat enough food and get enough sleep to keep growing, and to establish a baseline of peace in the household.

To me, my Mom's rules sounded a little like this...

I felt like bedtime should be a flexible time frame. Absolutely not.

I wanted a snack, seemingly always 20 minutes before a meal. And ruin your dinner?

I pushed back against chores—wasn't my mom home all day to do those things? Ummm...that did not go over well.

And then some rules, well...they were uniquely Mom.

I wanted to wear white before Easter, or after Labor Day. What could you be thinking?

I longed to learn how to cook, by her side. Way too messy.

I wanted to have friends over spontaneously, without a plan for dinner, transportation, or entertainment. No ma'am.

If I wore pearls with jeans, I was sent back upstairs to change because Pearls are for after 5 p.m. and jeans are not.

We lived at our lake home in the summer, which meant we also lived in our bathing suits. But wet bathing suits were only allowed in certain parts of the house. This is how we keep nice things nice.

And often, when we had company or went to someone's home for dinner, Mom would hold my little chin in her hands, look me straight in the eye and remind me that Children are to be seen and not heard. I was horrible at this one.

I have already said this, but it is worth repeating. I am confident that while my mother's rules felt confusing and unpredictable to me as a child, I know she was doing her absolute best. Because of her own mother's death at a much too early season of her life, the world felt unmanageable to her and enforcing tight guidelines was how she was going to keep us protected. The problem is, no matter how many guardrails you put up, sometimes someone you love reaches for a snack and dies on the toll road in Ohio. Or your fifteen-year-old child gets diagnosed with Cancer. Life and the people in it cannot be controlled by us (or our rules) and this was a difficult truth for Mom to accept and live by. She was, after all, only 26 when her mother died. That left a lot of years to live without the person who carried you into being and influenced you in ways only a mother can.

I didn't know anything about my Grandma Royer and the trauma her death caused Mom when I was four or eight or even when I was twenty. What I did know was that I was a kid who needed A LOT and I wanted mom to give it to me in a particular way: snuggles, bedtime stories, sitting on the floor and playing, or standing next to her in the kitchen while she cooked dinner. For reasons I was never able to understand, she wasn't able to express her love and affection for me in that way. She expressed love through a clean and well-appointed home, through dinner at 6 p.m. sharp with everything hot on the table at the same time, through loving Dad for over 60 years, through a giddy joy about Christmas, through a love for all things beautiful (most especially flowers), and more. There's a Buddhist saying that says, "We learn intimacy on the laps of our mothers." As a kid, I didn't really care how clean the bathrooms were, I just wanted to be scooped up and held in my mother's lap.

I have thought for a long time that when my mom lost her mom, it knotted her up inside in ways that would stay tangled for years. No amount of love from Dad or us three kids or even her faith in God would be able to do the untangling. That wouldn't come until she was dying, and it was a sight to behold.

In the summer of my mom's 83rd year, she had her own massive coronary on the front porch of our lake home. Only Dad and my sister-in-law were around, and it was traumatic for everyone involved. 911 was called, and because our summers are spent in a pretty small town, Mom was life-lined to the big city. The morning after her heart "event" (that's what they call them now in case you wondered), it was just Mom and I in her room as the cardiologist came to draw us a picture of the damage to her heart. He told her that the damage had been severe, and her heart would not survive another "event," and because of her age and the weakened state of her body, the likelihood for another event was pretty high. She told the 40-years-her-junior doctor that she wasn't worried and told him that she did not want any heroic efforts taken in the case of a subsequent attack. My mother looked around the room, out the window at the rising sun, at my face, and then looked right at Dr. C and said, "There are things for me to do and I can't get them accomplished here." This is when I knew something had shifted and that in all likelihood, my mother was dying.

We would have her just one more month after that first "event." She left the hospital after two weeks and spent two more weeks in rehab. We all felt that it was important that Mom was not alone. So, my sister who had come from Kansas, my dad, and my brother all spent the day shift with Mom, and my husband and I came after supper and would stay with her until bedtime. We established a routine: we would listen to some music, watch the sunset outside her bedroom window, get her ready for bed, read the Jesus Calling devotional for the day, pray with her, and then turn the lights out and head home. One of these nights I was laying on her bed, my head resting in her lap—the very place I had longed to be for nearly all of my 55 years —and I asked her if she was worried. "Oh no," she said, "I'm not worried about a thing." I looked over at my husband who was facing both of us across the room and sent him a, "What the heck, did you just hear that?" look. Because Mom was a worrier. She worried about her children, her in-law's children, her children's children. She worried about the state of affairs in the world, the poor, the abandoned, the African village with no clean water, single moms on their own, and she worried about how she was going to arrange the furniture so the whole family could eat Christmas dinner in the same room.

She. Worried. About. Everything.

So, I pushed her a bit, "Mom, so you're not worried about anything? Not the grandkids or dad or dying?" "Nope," was her quick reply. And then I took what felt like a risk. Mom had worried plenty about our oldest, Benjamin. He was the only black child in a family of white people. He struggled in high school and we were all concerned he wouldn't graduate. He got arrested in the winter of his Junior year and struggled to find his way back to joy. He went to college and flunked out. He started and stopped a lot of jobs, looking for some kind of fulfillment that seemed to be alluding him. He lived on his own, moved home, lived on his own again, and then moved back home. Mom saw much of this, some of it I chose not to share because it was difficult to know what her reaction might be. From what she saw though, Mom was concerned for Ben and his future, and she shared that worry with me often. So, when I asked Mom about her concern for Ben on this post-heart event day, she responded with, "Oh honey," she said, "he's going to be fine in ways you just can't see yet." You can bet I was a bit surprised.

We finished our routine, tucked her in, hugged and kissed her, and said good-night and as we were walking to the car, I began weeping and I said to my husband, "My mother is dying, she must be peeking into heaven or something because that not worrying thing, that is not her."

She would be gone six days later.

I shared in the chapters on Faith that there was a season in my early forties when I started to spiral spiritually as I ran smack into the intersection of my need to please all the people around me and my inability to do so.

The three hooligans put in my care to raise were having the audacity to act their ages (14, 13, and 9) and that's just a parenting conundrum that everyone I know struggles to sort out.

My friends seemed to need something from me that for the life of me I didn't know how to access or offer.

My boss kept moving the target on what it meant to be "effective" in ministry and so everything inside of me just knew that I had NOT heard God's call on my life correctly.

My mom and I had a beast of a fight over something so small and seemingly insignificant that it felt like a confirmation to the voice that had taken up residence in my head a long time ago: that I would never be able to meet her standards.

Failing everywhere. At least that's what it felt like. Looking back, I know that was not actually true, but you couldn't have convinced me of that then. I was doing everything I knew to do, short of literally jumping through hoops, and still falling desperately short in the "making the people in my life happy" category.

So, I did the only thing I knew to do when I got to the end of myself, I went for a walk.

Miles of walking was happening during this season.

And it was during one of these treks when I felt the prompting to get back into a rhythm doing the OTHER thing I knew to do when life got hard—call my therapist.

I'm a big believer in therapy. Solid, faith-based counsel has, for me, been a lifeline back to level ground over and over again in my life. And this time was no different. Within just a few weeks, I remembered what I have long known was true, but forgot: *I can't make people happy. They have to choose that for themselves.*

I could either keep trying to stay on that people-pleasing treadmill OR I could actually show up as my true self in all the places where I needed to be.

Even though I had been in and out of counseling for over 15 years by then, I was finally getting down to the truth inside of me that could counter the lie that, "Children should be seen and not heard," which I had long interpreted as, "Your voice, your presence, your opinion isn't needed here" or, more crassly, "Sit down and shut up." Which, as you could guess, led to some people-pleasing tendencies.

It wasn't enough anymore to be charming and winsome and funny so people would be happy with me, I needed to actually show up as me. Opinionated, sometimes too loud, and always full of energy—but with a voice of wisdom and a heart that can love BIG. A heart that can still disagree with you and can walk away still friends, even if you aren't happy with me.

It was an unraveling of years of living a particular way, but in the end, I felt a kind of "freedom to be" with others that I had only ever experienced with my husband. I was different and if it didn't show on the outside, I was OK with that. I knew what was true inside of me and how it was changing the way I was present in every relationship I was in.

About a year before Mom died, she and I were in a really good place. It was easier between us and when it did get a bit "tangly," I was self-aware enough to know what was mine to be responsible for between us and what was not. It felt like all kinds of liberation and joy—peace that passes understanding. I mentioned this to my therapist and her response was, "You watch, Suze. When it is time for your mom to die, your grief will be the grief of a daughter losing her mother, not that of a daughter with a bunch of unresolved 'stuff.'" So, as my gut and heart knew Mom was dying and I was telling Kelly that very thing, my mind went back to my therapist's words, and I knew she would be right. Because I had done the necessary work around what I was contributing to the complicated parts of my relationship with Mom, my grief has been filled with missing her and her beauty and love and her tell-it-like-it-was approach to life.

At the end of my mom's life, all that rule-making and rule-keeping and all the worrying and the trying to protect us just fell away, and all that was left was Mom. The purest version of my mother was the mother I got those last five weeks. Without a need anymore for rules or guardrails, the end was in sight for her, and what she saw there was good.

I could not be more humbled and grateful to have gotten to be with my mom as she slipped from this life into her real Home. Walking straight into the arms of Jesus first and then into her mother's embrace, I'm sure she got to hear, "You made it Mimmie, it's so good to have you Home." Being with Mom as she was dying felt holy and sacred and intimate and so, so sad. I felt all of it. All that was complicated between us was there, but now it lived way in the background of our reality. It wasn't a case of glossing over the years of contention, it was about freedom to love Mom in the way I was meant to love her. I'm pretty confident that would not have been true for me if I had never confronted the lie that my voice didn't matter and I should just sit down and be quiet.

Do I wish she would have found the freedom she had at the end sooner? Sure. Did I spend a big chunk of my life longing for her to say to me, just once, "Beloved daughter of mine, you know all those times I told you children should be seen and not heard? Ignore that. I didn't know what I was talking about. Your voice does matter. I was just so scared of so many things, and I was trying to control what I could. And you got hurt by that and I'm sorry?" Or something like that? Yes. I did.

I DO wish she could have found the joy that comes from laying down false thinking earlier, because so many people in her orbit would have benefitted from that journey. But actually, I wish it more for her than for me. I think about all the angst she felt over the years because one of us (or someone at church or even the manager at the local department store) wasn't following one of her rules. All the times she could have chosen to "go with the flow," but instead she chose to get angry or hurt and then withdraw.

Here's what I know now, after three years of being motherless— my mother loved me deeply and if the world wouldn't have broken her heart over and over, I bet she could've held mine a little more tenderly.

Oh, and P.S. I asked my daughters, who are now in their twenties themselves, and they said I could tell you that I've been a pretty great Mom. Not perfect (um, rude!), but just right for them.

And the next time I see my mom, I'll tell her the very same thing.

TO CONSIDER

What lie have I believed about my relationship with my mother (or prominent parental figure), either about myself or them?

What truth could replace this lie?

What will knowing this truth change about the way I'm living?

Because change isn't a solo undertaking, who, among my trusted friends can I tell about this discovery?

Exhibit B: "Alone" Isn't Such a Bad Word

Harvard recently published a study about the percentage of people in America who are lonely.[2] I used to do some research as a part of my work life and I could probably read all the tables and reports and data in the study, but do I need to? I don't think we need an ivy-league study to tell us we are lonely people. One in three adults and over half of women with young children according to that Harvard study reported feeling "seriously lonely."

These results are concerning but not surprising. As well, I think the world-wide health crisis (COVID 19) we are just now starting to emerge from has changed us, profoundly. It's my belief that so many were already deeply and heartbreakingly lonely BEFORE the pandemic, and then add all the isolation and withdrawal and fear and political division and, well...too many of us now find ourselves feeling invisible and alone. Even if we are back to work or church and are tempted to believe that our emptiness can be filled by living big chunks of our lives "publicly" on social media, this loneliness is just part of our realities.

Relationships at their core have always been a mystery to me. I was born into a loving family where I was cared about and for. I have had good friends and I think I have been a good friend. I had a couple serious dating relationships and one that developed into my forever teammate. My children have become adults that I love sharing life with, well beyond a parent/child thing. And yet, as I write this, I can easily access a kind of ache inside me that I'm sure that I'm convinced can only be filled by a longing for a kind of "nearly impossible for me to chase down" relational connection. Like a well worn rut in the road, either my heart or my head has often ended up in this empty space that seems like it ought to be filled by a relationship of some kind. When I was single, I was sure a husband would fill this hole in me. When I was childless, my heart told my head that a baby would fix it once and for all. Then, after the babies came, and the emptiness remained, I also thought maybe spending time building relationships with other young moms would solve it. But, as time has marched forward and all the realities of my life have continued to change like a revolving door in the entrance of a fine hotel—the belief has remained: Something is wrong, way down in the essence of who I am, that keeps me from building and maintaining deep relationships.

Thoughts about my relational world and the way I perceive my "lack" or inability to cultivate and nurture friendships often hit me at two in the morning, when my aging body and overactive imagination wake me up like I've slept a full eight hours and it's time to get up. However, when I take that belief of a flaw in my relational building ability out into the light of day, I can see it for the lie it is. While I'm nowhere close to perfect when it comes to being with people, I have confidence I do know how to do relationships with kindness and love, and the evidence is in the names of my husband, our grown children, and a few dear friends. So, what is it then that has been chasing me all these years? This longing for "true" and "real" and "deep," something that when I think about it, I can't identify a time I have lived without, but the fulfillment to it has remained just out of reach.

I think part of it is my personality, which is not necessarily unique to me, but is uniquely me, and part of it is pretty common.

The common part? Well, like a toddler standing at the top of the slide waiting for her parent's full attention before starting her descent—we are all born with a desire to be seen, known, and chosen for who we are. For some of us, that need is met instantly and completely in our earliest years, we have a sense of belonging from the beginning and this awareness of being "known" bears the kind of fruit in a child that nourishes their ability to be fully content in relational plenty or "want." Others of us, for reasons we have no control over, arrive in places with people who are on their own journey of longing to be seen and known and consequently, have a harder time offering that to others, even their children. My perspective on my formative years story is the latter.

The personality part is complicated. In fact, it seems that being "me" has proven to be a bit of a conundrum for many (and by many, I mean everybody but my husband). I am an extrovert who likes to be by herself. I want to be helpful but can get tangled up in how the "help" I offer to others makes me feel about myself and then it ends up not being very helpful for anyone. I have a TON of feelings, about ALL the things, but sometimes I can be very unsure what I am actually feeling. I want to belong in every setting I find myself in, but am so convinced that there is something unfixable and broken buried inside me that I don't, by default, bring my whole self to the relationship. Consequently, I often end up feeling like an outsider looking in. The result of living like this has been that I can be in a room full of people or sitting across from a friend sharing coffee and feel indescribably desolate and lonely.

Complicated.

When I was in my early fifties I found myself alone and confused on a journey into a relational "desert." To be sure, I had quite unintentionally chosen this for myself. I had left a job I enjoyed with people I cared deeply about and I didn't have another job to go to. It was a ministry position and leaving that kind of work, no matter what the reasons, can be really difficult. As the kids these days say, IYKYK.

As the weeks without work turned into months, I began to lose my "way." As in, I second guessed every decision I had made that got me to that jobless state. "Had I really heard from God or was I just tired?" "If it was the right decision, why did I feel so lonely in it?" "Why was I being punished if it really was what I was supposed to do?" "Was I being punished?" I had more questions than answers and the God who had so clearly and LOUDLY told me to resign, seemed to be offering only silence when I asked Him, "What now?" To make matters more intense, most of the folks I had worked with or been in relationships with were in turbulent water themselves. There was a senior leadership change happening and there were plenty of challenges for everyone. It felt like every time I reached for a helping hand, those hands were paddling furiously to keep their own dear selves above the waterline of survival.

For someone like me, who values that whole being seen, known, and chosen thing...this was a perfectly imperfect storm. What had begun as a step of faith, quickly turned into a long, heartbreaking wandering into the desert of shame, confusion, and loneliness. The longer I stayed on that path, the more alone and abandoned I felt.

Here's the thing about this season of my life, I was never really alone. I had a child still at home, I was married to a man who absolutely understood the journey I was on, I had a therapist who I was meeting with regularly, and I have a Heavenly Father who promises me I will never be alone. But, as it is sometimes when life gets complicated, the people I wanted to understand and "be with" me on that tough part of my journey, just weren't able to. They were all going through their own "stuff" and were unavailable to me in the ways I thought I longed for.

"I had more questions than answers and the God who had so clearly and LOUDLY told me to resign, seemed to be offering only silence when I asked Him, 'What now?'"

As the months went on, I got more despondent and discouraged. Every session with my therapist I asked her, "Do you think I'm depressed?" and her response would be, "No, I think you're lonely and sad." Until month twelve, when I asked her and her response that time was, "Yes, I think you are depressed." We walked through the rubric that therapists use to tell the difference between melancholy and actual clinical depression and I checked just about every box. According to my therapist, I had stayed in that "desert" of lonely, sad, and confused long enough to change my brain chemistry and the result was I was no longer just sad, I was depressed. I met with my family physician and he prescribed an antidepressant and, hallelujah, it worked. Fourteen days after swallowing that first pill, the fog began to lift and my heart felt lighter.

With a greater sense of clarity, I stayed in therapy but now the focus was sorting out whatever it was the sadness, confusion, sense of abandonment, and depression had been trying to convince me of. First thing on the list, there's a difference between lonely and alone. For me, being lonely is a feeling I experience when I feel abandoned or betrayed or if I stay isolated with myself for too long. Being alone is simply me just being by myself. This differentiation would prove to be a pivotal learning for me in that season, an awakening that may not seem like that big a deal to some, but for me was the invitation out of the desert: Being lonely and being alone are two very different realities and neither one is going to kill me.

Understanding the difference between those two was life-changing for me. When my heart and my head can hold onto the truth that I'm never really alone, and for sure never abandoned, then being lonely can do its job as a symptom of something else and being all by myself can be restorative in ways I hadn't imagined it could be.

For instance, recently our whole family, minus one who couldn't make it home, was gathered together at our lake home. There were 26 of us at every meal, playing in the water, competing in a family wiffleball tournament, and eating more snacks than I care to count. Then, all of a sudden, everyone left to go back to their lives in the "real" world and I stayed behind to do some laundry, straighten up the place, clean out the leftovers—all the things you do after you've had a houseful of love and laughter and eating. As I was going about my clean up routine, it hit me that I was all by myself. At first, I was glad for the break from the noise and the meal prep and, well...the noise. But then, the loneliness started to creep in and my heart began to ache for all those boisterous, hungry family members of mine. However, before it took control of my heart and head, I sat down with myself and asked, "What are you actually longing for?" and here's what I sensed—I was missing my Mom and Dad. We had just all gathered for the first time since Mom and Dad had died and their absence was like a giant chuckhole in the road, no matter how I tried to maneuver around it, it just could not be avoided.

Maybe loneliness is meant to help me see something that needs to be uncovered or changed in my life, but if I'm not paying attention

I'll never discover what it is. I am aware there are things about myself I would never know if I hadn't first been lonely. Being lonely is unsettling for me and so I avoided it for a long time. I also think loneliness is upsetting and disruptive culturally and so we have created and participated in a lot of activities so that we are never truly alone or lonely.

One of the ways I tried to avoid loneliness was by making sure I was always busy in my relational world. I made coffee dates, filled the calendar with family or friends over for dinner, or planned an activity with a friend. While I enjoyed all those gatherings, my motives were "off," I wasn't spending time with people so I could just be with them, building a relationship. I was filling my calendar and drinking gallons of coffee so I wouldn't have to be alone with me.

I've been in a committed relationship to the same amazing human for 38 years. We dated for two of those years and have been married for the rest. When we stood in front of our friends, family and God to exchange our wedding vows I had no idea that we were actually going to live those out.

"Kelly, I choose you above all others, to be my wedded husband,
to have and to hold from this day forward,
for better, for worse,
for richer, for poorer,
in sickness and in health,
to love and to cherish,
till death do us part,
according to God's holy ordinance; and thereto I pledge thee
my faith."

All of that has happened, except that "till death do us part," but that's on its way someday as well.

The point here is that while I have had the honor of being in a marriage where I have been chosen over and over again, where we have been rich (not really) and poor (really), where we've seen better days and some "worse" ones too, where there's been plenty of sickness and even some years of health, and I have felt loved and cherished...

I have still been lonely.

Plenty.

That loneliness, when I've let it, has taught me things about my married self. Through the feeling of loneliness, I have had to ask what is it that the loneliness is trying to point out in me? Curiously, the loneliness in my marriage has taught me two primary things:

1. Kelly was not meant to meet all my relationship needs.

2. Being alone is actually important for my overall health.

I am mentally, physically, and spiritually stronger if I take the time to be by myself, whether it's an hour walk at the end of the day or three days away somewhere by myself. In his book, *Sacred Marriage*, Gary Thomas presents the idea that maybe marriage isn't about our happiness. Rather, Thomas suggests that marriage has always been about our journey toward holiness.[3] I think that's true. Marriage was never meant to guarantee we weren't lonely, it was meant to make sure there was someone there to walk with us when the loneliness comes, reminding us that "lonely" is just a feeling and being alone isn't always a bad thing.

As I'm writing this, our three beautiful, smart, witty, and almost always full of passion children are all single. If they long for the partnership that marriage could bring them, I hope the Lord gives them that. If they want to be married because they're counting on it to stave off the ache of loneliness, my prayer for them would be to get that sorted out first. For the record, I love being married. I'm convinced that these nearly 40 years with Kelly Fair have made me more of who I was always meant to me. But I'm not counting on him to protect me from ever feeling alone or abandoned. What I'm counting on him for is to walk with me when I do.

I also love having friends who know my whole story and a community where I feel like I can belong and make a contribution. However, while that's true I have also felt profoundly lonely in these places. These relationships, just like my relationship with Kelly, were never meant to define me, to impart value or worth on me, or to guarantee a "place" for me because I was in them.

I carry with me now, since that difficult desert season, the profound "knowing" that I can experience a deep and achy loneliness and not die. I can find my way by myself (even though I'll never turn down a helping hand) because the kinship I'm longing for comes not from the person I am married to or through any other relationships I'm in, but rather from someone and someplace else entirely—from the One who, from the beginning of my time has been saying, "that Suze girl, she's pretty spectacular because she's mine." Period.

TO CONSIDER

What lie have I believed about my experience with feeling alone/abandoned or lonely?

What truth could replace this lie?

What will knowing this truth change about the way I'm living?

Because change isn't a solo undertaking, who, among my trusted friends can I tell about this discovery?

Exhibit C: We Really Are Better Together. Really.

A couple weeks ago, there was a group of beautiful people from our church at our table. This is a new-ish community of faith for us and honestly, getting to know people has been challenging. Not because the people are difficult, but the circumstances sure have been. This is a church plant from a larger congregation, so there were some existing relationships to try and find our footing in, we went through the "worship from home" challenges that COVID-19 caused, and we don't work there, which, for a family that has spent 30 of the last 35 years on staff at a church, getting to know folks when you're not there to "work" is a big deal. But it's happening, slowly but surely, and mostly at a table somewhere. So, this group—Black, White, Latino, young, old, male, female, married, single—were gathered at our table and we were checking in, seeing how everyone was doing since we'd last been together. One of the gentlemen (Henry) was sharing that as he neared retirement age, he's finding himself wondering (maybe even a bit worried) if he has "enough" set aside to stop working. This seemed like a reasonable and logical lament and several at the table were resonating with it. After Henry shared his concern, an already retired gentleman (Jim) at the end of the table pulled out his wallet and handed Henry a $2 bill. "I carry several of those with me all the time and anytime I run into someone who's questioning if they have enough, I give them one. Because where two or more are gathered, God is there too." Jim went on to say that he had given them to waitresses, college kids, neighbors, and now Henry. As Henry tried to hand it back, Jim said, "No brother, you keep that and when you see it, remember God's got you now and in whatever is coming." I was wavering between sobbing and breaking into laughter because of all the joy that was trying to burst out of my heart.

That exchange might have happened if the two men had run into each other after church and had that conversation—but this night, because we were gathered at the table, everyone there got to be a part of it—inspired by the faith and generosity of one brother to another. The youngers were wide-eyed and wondering and those of us "middlers" were reminded, yep, God's got us too. I wanted to ask Jim for my own $2 bill, but felt like that might be a little much. Instead, I was left in awe of the power of community.

Community is hard for me. As I've already shared, I can tend to be a bit of a chameleon when it comes to being with people—I'm an introverted extrovert who longs to be in authentic relationships with others but gets overwhelmed by what that requires and tends to pull back and isolate. It's complicated for me, but over the years I've had people care about me enough to lovingly challenge me to keep pursuing. It's imperative that I belong to other people, it matters deeply to my well-being and it's hard as hell.

25 years ago, our little family moved back to the part of the country I grew up in. We chose a house that was in an older part of town, had the room we needed, and was affordable for us. It felt kind of risky for two "kids" who had grown up in subdivisions, but we loved the character of the home and the front-porch vibe of the street. We were naive enough to think we were just moving into a house. Instead we moved into a neighborhood—a place where everyone would learn your name and lend a helping hand if your life circumstances required it. We lived on that street for 23 years and every one of those years was crammed with days and weeks and moments where our neighbors transitioned into our friends. These were the people who fed us, watched our kids, mowed our grass, helped paint the house (more than once), took in our mail while we were on vacation, chased the dog when he bolted out the front door, and loaned us their electricity when the power went out. We've been to graduations and weddings and funerals with these folks, and when it was time to move, it felt as if we left part of our physical bodies behind.

In year six of living there, we decided to remodel our one and only full bathroom. Please keep in mind: we are not DIY-ers, and this was in the days before YouTube, Pinterest, or Google—we were in way over our heads. We had no idea what we were doing and called on the kindness of others to get us through. From start to finish, that project took 13 weeks. Three months without a bathtub or shower with three small children—please think about that for a minute. After a week or two of bathing at my parents (which was 15 minutes away), we realized this was not sustainable and so, we asked our next door neighbors if we could shower at their house. They said, of course (because they're generous like that), and for the next 11 weeks, I took the kids to Grandma's for a bath in the evening and then in the morning, Kelly and I walked across the side yard, with toiletries and clothes in hand, let ourselves in the Bobay's back door, went upstairs, and took our showers. Years later, we were out to eat with these neighbor-friends and we were remembering that season of life. As we retold the story, I got to the part where I said, "Can you believe we did that for three months?" They looked at us with utter disbelief on their faces. They thought we had done the whole borrowing of the shower deal for a week or two. They had no idea it was a quarter of the calendar. That right there is good neighboring.

My husband and I have met and become friends with a lot of people over the nearly 40 years we have been a team. But it was this neighborhood, these neighbors, that actually taught us what it meant to belong somewhere outside our families. To have people who see you at your best (and worst), who hear you lose it with your kids (thank you small yards and open windows in the Spring), cover for you when life is out of control, invite you to come over and throw something on the grill and share a meal, and show up in the big and small moments of your life is a gift I didn't even know I needed to ask for. The generosity of that community and the sense of belonging I felt there would stay with me after we moved and entered a new, more difficult season of community.

As you already know, my Mom had a massive coronary followed five weeks later by a stroke that would prove to be too much for her nearly 84-year-old body to hold up under. As she was in the last weeks of her life, it became clear to both Kelly and I that we were being called to sell our home on that street we loved, buy Mom and Dad's house, and ask my Parkinson's-diseased dad to stay and live with us. His relief was palpable and when I told mom, she managed to communicate, even though words were getting fewer and fewer, her understanding that we would take care of Dad. Before anyone celebrates this decision as altruistic or over-romanticize it as heroic, I want to tell you it's probably one of the most difficult things I've ever experienced.

We returned to our subdivision roots and it was a challenge. Not just the suburban life part, but the living with my dad part too. In the short time we lived together, I found myself challenged to practice what seemed to come so easily to our neighbors when they made us that three month loan of their shower—"If I have it and you need it, it's yours." This is a form of generosity that never fails to produce gratitude and honestly, I wish I had been more of a natural with it.

> "It's imperative that I belong to other people, it matters deeply to my well-being and it's hard as hell."

Honestly, when we moved in with Dad, I knew there might be some rough spots, but I didn't anticipate how difficult it would really be. He was, after all, grieving the loss of Mom and fighting a losing battle with a degenerative disease. I'm pretty sure I thought it was going to be the most natural thing for me to be generous and understanding all the time. Unfortunately, those thoughts of "ease" were wrong and while it was always rooted in love, our living situation proved to be pretty challenging—for everyone.

I've thought long and hard about why it was so difficult to all be under the same roof and the best I know to tell you is this: living with your parents, after not living with them for 40 years, is not for the faint of heart. Everyone has changed since the last time you were roomies, and even in the best of circumstances with the healthiest of relationships, there are going to be hard things. One of the challenges for me was confronting the mental story I had written about my dad throughout my life, and becoming aware that I may have gotten some details wrong.

I had spent the majority of my life painting a picture of my dad with a pretty broad brush stroke: he was an excellent provider, devoted to my mother, committed to the church, and loved few things more than having his kids and grandkids around him. As we lived together, I began to observe and experience some of the finer details of my Dad and his personality—things I wouldn't have seen or encountered in the four decades I had been building a life of my own (which, trust me, is plenty full of "finer" details) separate from him. None of the ways Dad lived his life that I began to find irksome or the parts of his personality that proved to be somewhat irritating as we lived together, were things he didn't have a right to. These were characteristics and traits that he and Mom had sorted out in their years of living together and it worked for them. Like me, he had a whole big life that he had built away from me. Suffice it to say that everyone in the household went through a learning curve of getting along as roommates, rather than just family who gathered for a meal or a game of cards every now and then.

I could make a list (and trust me, I've started plenty of them) of the things Dad did or said or the way he was that made it sometimes tough to live together, but what would be the purpose in that? For the most part, Dad was just being Dad, and as he aged and his health began to fail him, the energy he was using to "manage" the bits and pieces of his character that were not the best version of him was being diverted to the things that he once did without thinking about them—getting dressed in the morning, not falling down, and figuring out what it's like to be in the last chapter of the story of your life.

For 27 months, Dad shared living space in the home he and my mother built together that my husband and I now owned. Kelly and I often talked about the weight of responsibility we felt, living with Dad during his grief after losing the 64-year love of his life, selling his home, the progression of his disease, and the lockdown that came with a worldwide pandemic. But we also talked about the fact that this weight wasn't just ours, we knew we weren't alone in it. My brother and his wife, my sister and her husband, our kids, several additional grandkids willingly and often, jumped in to provide companionship and care for Dad.

Our lives changed profoundly in the years we lived with Dad. There was so much new and different and not quite "us" about this change in living arrangements it took us nearly a year to find a normal that seemed to work. Honestly, I spent more time than I'm proud of being frustrated with Dad or on edge about some comment or request. I often sensed my emotions rising in a moment and yet, felt I couldn't really get traction on moving beyond it. I was not offering the best version of myself to anyone during our first year together. I felt stingy and annoyed and downright sad—a lot. It's not that I didn't have understanding and compassion for all that Dad had lost, I did. I do, however, think my losses and sacrifices for the most part seemed invisible to him. His world had turned upside down, it was difficult for him to see that ours had too.

After the first year of trying to figure out all that was new and different (for both Dad and us) we did seem to find a normal that worked. We grew in our understanding of what it would mean to live well together. We started asking for time and space away from each other, I stopped suggesting to Dad that maybe a piece of pie and two cookies for breakfast wasn't his healthiest option, and Dad discovered he was not a fan of movies about Wizarding boys who wear glasses or a superhero who carries a giant hammer. We also learned that our family could keep living like we always had and Dad could either join in or not—no judgment either way. There was a kind of freedom that came from knowing our relationship would survive even when the conversations got uncomfortable, we didn't agree on politics, or the food I cooked seemed too "healthy" to him.

In the end, I was able to experience my Dad, the guy who had loved me for the whole of my life—not perfectly, but consistently and with gusto, with a kind of peace that can only come from God. I found my generosity and joyful heart and was able to say freely to him, "Dad, if you need it and I have it, it's yours."

I believe being housemates with Dad helped us all grow in a particular kind of knowledge about each other that can only come from living together (or at the very least spending a lot of time together): People are not always exactly who you think they are.

From a distance, it's easy to admire, like, or even want to emulate someone and the opposite can be true as well. It doesn't cost much to judge and criticize from far away. However, for us to know if that person is who they say they are, or even close to who we hope they are, we need to spend some time together. It's the very reason Jesus invited the 12 disciples to leave the families they knew and follow him. Jesus knew that if they were really going to be able to embrace who he was and what he was about, they were going to need to do more than see each other a couple times a year for a family get together. In order to decide if this was someone they could love with their whole lives and then take that love and pass it on, they would need to be with him, up close and personal, for an extended period of time (like say, three years).

A while ago there was a saying that became a kind of buzz phrase in the Church and in our culture too I guess, "We are better together." In theory, I think that's true. I agree with my friend Jim and his two dollar bill ministry—two ARE better than one. Many hands DO make light work. My neighborhood community was as special as it was because of how we came together. When we can practice kindness, empathy, and support together—it IS better. But what we don't talk about often enough is the cost of it all. To experience the power of "together" means I have to lay my own "stuff" (opinions, hurts, need to be right, etc.) down for a little bit, so that I can offer and receive differently. For the work to be lighter, I must be willing to ask for help and then take my pride and ego out of the equation and trust the outcome will be superior to what I could have achieved on my own. It was a profound sacrifice for those 12 young men to leave their families and be "together" with Jesus, it was a sacrifice to live with my dad, and it was also a privilege that changed me forever.

Dad's gone now. He died 30 months after Mom did, right after a Thanksgiving celebration where nearly his whole family was around him. Even though we didn't know it was near the end, we knew he was failing and so for the few months leading up to Thanksgiving, Dad had been living in a facility that could provide him more care than the family was able to. For the last three months of his life, I wasn't my Dad's roommate—I was his daughter. What a gift that proved to be. Someone else could change the bandages and manage the meds and clean up after him. I could just be with him and remember that as perfectly imperfect as he was—he was exactly the right Dad for me. He was mine and I was his and belonging to him brought with it a lot of joy. I'm glad I got to remember that before he left this temporary home to go to the place where he actually belonged. We WERE better together and I'll miss that we won't be able to be that way again until I join him and Mom someday in Heaven.

Until then, I want to get better at this generous and costly way of living that so many (including Dad) have modeled for me. I want to be an "if I have it and you need it—it's yours" wife, mother, sister, friend, and Jesus person.

P.S.

I know I said I wouldn't share any lists concerning Dad, I do however, want to say this, my Dad was a bit of a slob. Which my mother used to talk about (a lot) and I would always defend Dad, saying something like, "Mom, you're so hard on him, it can't be that bad."

Ummm...

Dear Mom, I'm sorry. You were right, it was that bad.

TO CONSIDER

What lie have I believed about "community" (a place where you belong and others belong to you) and my place in it?

What truth could replace this lie?

What will knowing this truth change about the way I'm living?

Because change isn't a solo undertaking, who, among my trusted friends can I tell about this discovery?

Exhibit D: Turn Up the Communication

When I was a kid, my parents bought the coolest family car of all time ever (at least to my elementary age self). It was a brand new fully equipped, which included a rear-facing third row seat, turd brown station wagon. That station wagon was the first brand new car I have memory of my folks purchasing and it was awesome. When I got dibs on the back seat, it was as if I was in my own little travel bubble. Just me and the cooler full of bologna sandwiches on white bread, staring out the window of where we had been. Back then, before middle age messed up my inner ears, I could read for hours in the car and that's what I did, for miles and miles I read and snuck pretzel sticks out of the snack bag.

As a family, we only took a couple really long road trips a year. Mom's family lived in Pennsylvania so we frequently traveled east right after Christmas, and Dad's parents spent November through May in Florida, so often we headed south in the spring. Other than life in my third row cocoon, my other strong memories from those trips over the years was that sometimes my mom would not talk for hours. When this happened, I knew she wasn't sleeping, she seemed, for the most part, mad. She was turned a little to the right, elbow on the door, hand under her chin, staring out the window, in silence. For hours.

Now, as a nearly 60-year-old woman, I understand she was most likely pissed at Dad. I'm guessing it had something to do with plans being changed, or chaos around getting three kids and all the "stuff" out the door on time, or some other kind of exchange that happens between spouses when you get crammed in the car with your children, the luggage, the cooler, and everyone's expectations for the trip. But as a kid, and a pretty sensitive one at that, I was absolutely convinced that I was the cause of those silences. I would spend her hours of silence wondering what I had done to make her so angry. Decades later, she and I talked about it. She couldn't ever really pinpoint a reason for those stoic hours, but she did remember them, and assured me they weren't connected to me.

I wish I could have learned that lesson ("It's not about you Suze") then, as an eight or nine-year-old child. Instead, I became a sensitive soul who was pretty sure most everyone was mad at me or talking about me or plotting against me, most of the time. Instead of just asking the assumed antagonist if what I thought was happening was actually happening, "Did I do something to offend you?" I just operated like it was true and ended up causing a lot of pain along the way.

Here's the irony, I have a graduate degree in Communication and have taught the subject at the University level and yet, I can still trip all over myself sometimes when it comes to clearly and honestly communicating. For as long as I can remember, I've worried about my voice being heard. What I know now, but didn't always, is that I've carried a deep worry that no one actually wants to hear from me or understand my point of view. This worry turns into fear and as the fear of being silenced, misunderstood, or dismissed grows, I tend to choose a petty, unobliging, and unhelpful approach to communication. I can presume people know what I'm talking about when they don't, I can talk too fast, I can interrupt, be arrogant, get my feelings hurt, not close the loop on hard things after they're resolved, and I can withdraw and go silent—just like Mom.

The only solution I've discovered for blunders in communication is actually more communication, and not in the "I'll just keep talking until you understand me" kind of way. But rather, in a "I really want to understand what you're saying so I'm going to shut up and let you talk" kind of way. For me, what seems to bring clarity and resolution to these communication trip ups, and there have been plenty, is when I chose humility and curiosity. When I listen more than I talk, when I offer what I'm thinking and feeling when all I really want to do is clam up, when I ask questions rather than offer opinions, and when I worry less about getting my point across and instead, try to hear (as in really hear) what the other person is trying to communicate.

There's a beautiful anonymously written prayer, often wrongly attributed to St. Francis of Assisi, that articulates more clearly than I ever could about this idea of staying curious and humble when it comes to communicating with others:

> *Lord, make me an instrument of your peace.*
> *Where there is hatred, let me bring love.*
> *Where there is offense, let me bring pardon.*
> *Where there is discord, let me bring union.*
> *Where there is error, let me bring truth.*
> *Where there is doubt, let me bring faith.*
> *Where there is despair, let me bring hope.*
> *Where there is darkness, let me bring your light.*
> *Where there is sadness, let me bring joy.*
> *O Master, let me not seek as much*
> *to be consoled as to console,*
> *to be understood as to understand,*
> *to be loved as to love,*
> *for it is in giving that one receives,*
> *it is in self-forgetting that one finds,*
> *it is in pardoning that one is pardoned,*
> *it is in dying that one is raised to eternal life.*
>
> ANONYMOUS[4]

This is what I know, but don't always remember, there will always be time to be understood. Always.

However, if time runs out, then my opinions and ideas and "whatever the heck it was I was trying to say," will just have to stay unsaid. If I'm not willing to set myself and my need to be heard aside long enough to try and understand someone else's point of view or opinion or even choices, then it is clear I have an issue with humility on top of lacking some communication skills.

I think this is what Jesus was talking about when he said, "The last will be first and the first will be last." In Matthew's telling of the Good News, we read a story that Jesus told about a landowner who needed to hire workers for his vineyard. He hired workers in the morning, at noon, and then with just one hour to go in the work day and then at the end of the day, that landowner paid them all the same. The ones hired the earliest got angry of course, they deserved more for working longer, but that's not the way Jesus told the story. The landowner was being generous and the workers couldn't see it because of their need for what they saw as inequity. "That's not fair?" it seems they were clamoring, "We were here first, and we should get more." However, that doesn't seem to be the way it works in the Kingdom of God. The rules for equality have already been written and they can be found nailed to a cross.

I get it—it's scary to think there's no space for your voice or your ideas or your experience. The, "What about me?" mindset can be a taskmaster that's difficult to get out from under. However, if I am unwilling to trust that you want to hear what I have to say, that my thoughts on the "matter" hold value for you—then what is our relationship built on anyway?

"This is what I know, but don't always remember, there will always be time to be understood. Always. However, if time runs out, then my opinions and ideas and 'whatever the heck it was I was trying to say,' will just have to stay unsaid."

I've always known that words held power. The words we choose, the volume and the tone of how we say them, where we choose to say them, and when we decide to speak them, or not...all of that has power.

Other than being called in for dinner, I was never really yelled at as a kid. I do, however, know that the power of my parents' words (or lack of them) as they were directed toward me or about me, had a significant impact on my understanding of myself and our relationship. Just like a baby learns her name by the repetition of it, how we understand our own selves and our place in the world is shaped by some of the earliest words spoken over us. I had one parent who told me I could be and do anything I wanted, and I had another parent who told me they didn't know what they were going to do with me. These were confusing messages for me as a kid—did I have the potential to be and do a lot of great things or was I a bothersome pain in someone's rear-end? The answer to both questions is most definitely: Yes! But as a kid, I didn't yet understand that two things could be true. My little concrete mind was trying to figure out which of those messages I should believe and so, I chose the one that was easiest to believe—which, in my experience, has rarely been the positive message.

Words shape worlds and my world got shaped by plenty of early messages. Some were powerfully positive. I knew I was safe in my family, I was clear I was intelligent, and the love I felt from many was strong and supportive. However, I also was shaped by messages that ended up creating an ongoing sense inside of me that in order to be "OK" (with "OK" defined as liked, chosen, and part of the group) I would need to be unique, different, or special somehow. Like a ball and chain shackled to my leg, this message of nothing short of spectacular has been with me for a very long time. My memory is a little fuzzy, so the origin of it I'm not quite sure. I do remember feeling it in elementary school and beyond. I can positively tell you that after the very first Cancer, it was blasting into my heart and mind like it was coming through a megaphone. After all, you don't survive childhood Cancer just to become a run of the mill teenager or adult. It wasn't until I sat myself in a therapists' chair in my thirties, that I would unravel the lie about my worth and value that came wrapped inside the message that "normal" was a bad word and I needed to do everything in my power to not "settle" for average or "OK" in any area of my life.

Were people in my life like my parents, teachers, coaches, Sunday School teachers, trying to get me to believe that I had to be the best or one step above in order to belong? I have no idea. Maybe it was some kind of motivational strategy or maybe it was the way I interpreted the words I was hearing. Most of those people are gone now, so there's no going back and asking, "What in the heck were you trying to say to me?" Instead, I can be in charge of me and the meaning I made and hold onto from those words. As well, I'm in control of the words I choose to say to myself and others.

Unlearning something takes time and learning how to communicate beautifully and clearly and in an honoring way to the person you're communicating with is one of the hardest disciplines I know. When our kids were little, I worked hard at being mindful about the words I chose. However, based on conversations I have had with the adult version of the three of them, even when I thought I was offering the best I had in the moment, my words caused harm or the message I was sending got misinterpreted. It happens and it has an impact.

Have I gotten the choosing of words with intention wrong more than I've gotten it right? Absolutely. But I'm working on it. Especially when there's a particularly important conversation that needs to be had, I'm trying to remember, rather than just spouting off the first thing that comes to mind, to ask myself three questions:

1.   Is this the right thing to say?
2.   Is it the right time to say it?
3.   Is this the right place to say it?

If the answer to any of these three is "No," then I am learning to stop and regroup. What should I be saying? When would be a time to bring it up? Should this be a private conversation, or can we talk about this at the local coffee shop?

This approach has helped me in so many ways, in all the important conversations, easy and challenging, that I find myself in with people, because let's face it: it doesn't really matter how great you are at communication—difficult conversations are just difficult. So difficult in fact, that sometimes we avoid talking about the very thing we should be talking about and by avoiding the conflict (perceived or actual) we are in fact, creating more conflict.

I had a boss one time (well, more than one but that's for another chapter) who talked to me in a very condescending manner. For reasons I still don't understand—my gender, my education, my experience—he was constantly trying to put me down. It was really painful and frustrating, but I didn't say anything because, well...he was the boss. And yet, as his disrespectful approach continued and

I found myself talking "about" this guy, but not "with" him, I saw the relational hole I was digging. So, I gathered up the courage to talk with him. I shared how his words made me feel and how when he belittled me in front of the team that I felt disrespected. The conversation made my stomach hurt, but it went fine (and by fine I mean I didn't get fired) but something unlocked inside of me after I had that meeting. I knew, for sure, that it was time for me to leave that organization, and leaving when you're not angry or hurt or holding on to a bunch of unsaid things, is a great time to go. It felt like by laying down my avoidance and having the necessary conversation, I was able to clearly see the path was leading me out. Communication is like that—it can clear roadblocks and the air, in ways that avoiding never can.

As I've shared, at the end of her life, my mom and I were able to talk about a lot of things. I'm convinced that was because I had spent the last two decades being curious about her, fighting with her, making up, and most importantly talking with her about her life. I asked her about her decisions and her values. The things that brought her pain and gave her joy. We talked about her faith and her very complicated relationship with her own father. We had multiple conversations about all her rules and what flowers to plant and, yep, we talked about her car riding silence. I didn't always understand or agree with her answers—but at least we talked about it all. Because in the end, it wasn't about having the relationship all figured out, it was about embracing the love that was always true between us. As I watched her slip from our world into her actual home, I didn't have the regret of the unsaid that lots of people talk about having when someone they love dies. I'm grateful for that (thank you to my therapist) and want to keep living like that in all my relationships.

O Master, let me not seek as much
to be consoled as to console,
to be understood as to understand,
to be loved as to love,
for it is in giving that one receives,
it is in self-forgetting that one finds,
it is in pardoning that one is pardoned,
it is in dying that one is raised to eternal life.

ANONYMOUS[5]

TO CONSIDER

What lie have I believed about the importance of my voice when it comes to communicating with others?

What truth could replace this lie?

What will knowing this truth change about the way I'm living?

Because change isn't a solo undertaking, who, among my trusted friends can I tell about this discovery?

PART 4: WORK

LIE
Find something you love doing and you'll never work a day in your life.

TRUTH
Work is work and sometimes it's hard. However, we are created to make a unique contribution, something only we can do, and if we live like that, work won't ever define us or become our identity.

I have a very clear memory of being about 13-years-old (back before any child labor regulation) and asking my dad why I had to go back to my summer job. I hated it. I was washing dishes in the kitchen of a little diner, and it was hard work. It was also boring and hot, and I wanted to be anywhere but there on a sunny day in July. My dad listened to my lament and then looked me in the eye and said, "If it was supposed to be fun, they'd call it PLAY, Suze. Work is work—it's hard. Just wait until you find something you love doing, it won't feel like work at all."

That memory has stayed with me for nearly 45 years, mostly because I didn't agree with it then and I don't agree with it now. I have worked at a lot of things in a lot of places over the years. Sometimes I've loved what I was doing—couldn't wait to get there, hated to leave, and sometimes I have dreaded every one of the 480 minutes required for a full workday—either way, it is all still work.

If you want to know why work is often like holding onto a fistful of thorns and thistles, take a look at Genesis 3. In this third chapter of the very first book of the Bible, we see the origin story of why work is now what it was never meant to be—DIFFICULT. God intended our work, our labor if you will, to just be something we did to take care of the things we were meant to take care of, the earth, our animals, our families. Then, there was a garden and a snake and a woman and a temptation to "have it all", and an apple.

The words that follow are just my reflections on a BIG part of my life (work, career, vocation) that for many years I kept thinking was going to fill something up inside of me that it was never meant to fill. I spent nearly 30 years hoping my work would satisfy my longing for place, purpose, and belonging and it always fell short.

Today, my approach to work is different. To me, work is deeply satisfying (at times) and sometimes back-breaking, sweat-producing, heartbreaking, and frustrating as all get out. It is a place where I go to make a living to help provide for my family, live out of my calling, practice being a good human, lead when all I want to do is run, and be on the lookout for eternal moments, things that last way beyond any report or presentation or paycheck. Work plays a part in my life, but it does not get to define my life or me.

The evidence I present here is to rewrite the lie I lived by for years. Yes, find something you love doing, but be ready for those feelings to be temporary, and sometimes hard, and don't forget—your work does not define you and establish your worth. Only God gets to do that.

Our culture says that ruthless competition is the key to success.

Jesus says that ruthless compassion is the purpose of our journey.

BRENNAN MANNING[1]

Exhibit A: Who's Calling Please?

If you had asked me in my twenties what I felt like I was "called" to, I would have probably looked at you, cocked my head to the right a little bit and made up something clever (and by clever I mean the answer I thought you might be looking for) because I would have had no idea what you were talking about. Three decades ago, when I was in my early twenties I thought two things about calling, either: A) It was only for people who went into ministry, and B) that was never going to be me. What I didn't have clarity on then and would only gain through the wisdom and investment of others is that calling actually has very little to do with what I do, but everything to do with how and why I do what I do.

I graduated high school with dreams of becoming a lawyer, but quickly decided that was entirely too much work and money, so I redirected my dream and chose Business Management/Marketing. I wasn't really sure what to do, I was 18-years-old, with an 18-month-old driver's license in my wallet and the keys to the family's hand-me-down Toyota Corolla hatchback—what did I know about deciding what I wanted to DO when I grew up? So, I chose to major in Business. In 1983 there was no more generic major being offered and honestly, it felt like a "good enough" choice.

As I approached the end of my sophomore year, I knew Business was not for me. I didn't care enough about the policies and procedures and the strategy required to be successful in the world of marketing and management. The university had a really solid creative writing major and I wanted to explore that. However, when I broached this subject with my dad (who was paying the bulk of the bill) he quickly informed me that he wouldn't be supporting a change in majors. As I recall, I called him in tears after I had flunked a test in one of my marketing classes. It was actually my second F, but I had chosen not to tell him about the first one—too much shame—and so I'm not sure he really understood why I was so worked up. For him, I had flunked a test—no big deal; "It's good for you, everybody flunks, get that out of your system," was the essence of what I remember him saying. But I knew, way down inside me, that I was on the wrong path. When I asked him if I could switch majors and pursue something more creative, what I heard was, "Absolutely not." I had, after all, already invested two years of my time and their money on said marketing degree and my struggling a bit (ahem, flunking), was no reason to change horses midstream.

I respected my dad and trusted his wisdom and so I stayed the course with the business degree. Looking back, I should have trusted myself more. In 1984 people weren't having conversations about vocational calling, at least in my corner of the world, and so I thought "calling" was just a fancy way to say, "Find something you're really good at and do that." I didn't understand yet what I would come to believe with all my heart, that each of us has a unique contribution to make, that only that person can make. For instance, thousands of people feel a calling to be an educator. But only my sister could teach in the creative, caring, exciting way that Dawn Ellen Hoffman can teach.

Connecting with your calling is like tapping into a kind of deep joy that gets buried inside us, maybe before we even arrive on the planet, and then gets expressed in a variety of ways as we grow and learn and fail and get up and try again. Sometimes that deep joy gets expressed through work, but not always.

Whenever I talk with someone about their calling, or the place where that joy flows freely, I usually ask them, "When was the last time you thought, 'I was made for this?'" Like a signpost on a long road trip, those experiences help us know we're on the right path. I have rarely had those moments when I've been approaching work like I'm punching a time clock, instead they have come when I'm doing something creative or something connected to leading a team, or even better yet—when I'm doing something creative WITH a team.

After graduation, I stumbled around for years, working jobs in a variety of fields doing an even bigger variety of things. I've worked for profit and non-profit organizations and I've worked for myself. I've achieved some success in my career, as varied as it was. I was a supervisor, a team leader, a director, a manager and yet...I had very few "I was made for this" moments.

In the early 90s, I was handed my first Frederick Buechner book ironically by a client I was doing marketing consulting for, and that book changed my life. Buechner is in his 90s now and has written over 30 books. An ordained presbyterian minister, there is a winsomeness to his writing and his approach to the place where our faith intersects our work. When I turned the page in his book *Wishful Thinking: A Seeker's ABC* and read the words, I knew something needed to change when it came to my understanding of vocation:

> *"It comes from the Latin vocare, to call, and means the work a man is called to by God.*
>
> *There are all different kinds of voices calling you to all different kinds of work, and the problem is to find out which is the voice of God rather than of Society, say, or the Super-ego, or Self-Interest.*
>
> *By and large a good rule for finding out is this. The kind of work God usually calls you to is the kind of work (a) that you need most to do and (b) that the world most needs to have done. If you really get a kick out of your work, you've presumably met requirement (a), but if your work is writing TV deodorant commercials, the chances are you've missed requirement (b). On the other hand, if your work is being a doctor in a leper colony, you have probably met requirement (b), but if most of the time you're bored and depressed by it, the chances are you have not only bypassed (a) but probably aren't helping your patients much either.*
>
> *Neither the hair shirt nor the soft berth will do. The place God calls you to is the place where your deep gladness and the world's deep hunger meet."* [2]

I was not "glad," and as far as I could tell, there was no deep hunger from the world or myself being satisfied by the work I was doing. I had begun to lose my sense of self in my work, I was allowing it to define me and hoping it would impart a sense of value to my personhood. Rather than search for something I loved to do, I needed to seek out something I was called to do.

And so, I began to dream about what it would be like to listen, I mean really listen, to what God was saying to me about my vocational calling—and pursue that. Two things happened as I began to ask God what I should do, and both of them would point me in the direction of what I would soon discover was my actual calling. The first thing that happened was my friend and business partner Corinne and I got a call from the academic dean at Taylor University, who had a campus in Fort Wayne at the time. He had gotten our names from a former professor of mine who knew I was in the area and had some experience with marketing and marketing research as practitioners. Neither of us were teachers or even aspired to be, but it seemed like something that might be fun and challenging and so we said yes.

"Connecting with your calling is like tapping into a kind of deep joy that gets buried inside us, maybe before we even arrive on the planet, and then gets expressed in a variety of ways as we grow and learn and fail and get up and try again."

Corinne and I shared the load and we had a blast, even while we were trying to figure out how to grade papers and calculate grades fairly. Something sparked and came alive in me as I began to teach those college students. The second event was that Corrine and I, along with another partner, launched an audio magazine (think podcast before that was a thing) for women. We crammed as much content, interviews, music, bible memory, etc. as possible onto a CD-ROM, and then asked women to subscribe. We discovered so much about ourselves and our "deep joy" in this season, and lost a lot of money but that's a story for another time. We also discovered that it was time for both of us to step back from the business world and see what God had for us. Corinne would go on to be a pastor in Indianapolis and lead and shepherd hundreds of men and women, both here in the states and in Rwanda.

Me? I went back to school. After years of saying I was never going to be a teacher, it was the very thing my soul was longing to do. For the next decade I taught at that same small liberal arts Christian college where I first caught the teaching bug. Over the years, we had dozens of those students in our home and many became a part of our family. In this season, I would figure out that teaching was something I really enjoyed doing and I was good at it. I often drove home thinking, "That was a blast." And the audio magazine? Well, we've always said it was an idea before its time. It only lived for 2 ½ years, but it did spark in me the desire to explore my communication gift and it became the catalyst for my preaching and teaching in the local church and at conferences.

I still have so much to learn about discovering and leaning into my calling. In nearly 40 years of professional life, I have done a lot of things. Worked with some really great organizations and alongside some pretty amazing people. I have also found myself in a place where I didn't belong. Sometimes because I had outgrown the role, sometimes because I was scared to make a move, and sometimes it was because I had taken the easier path and ignored all the signs that a certain job or role did not align with my calling.

While "place" is something that matters profoundly both personally and professionally, I dare not let it define me. No matter what my title is, how much money I'm making, how many people report to me, or whether I feel my unique contribution and approach to living will bring value, this is not what establishes my worth. A job might be the result of being in the right place at the right time and I'm not talking about luck, I'm talking about occupying the space that has been set aside by God for me.

This brings me back to calling. Based on my experience, the truth about calling is there is one inside each of us and it has very little to do with what we're doing or where we're busy doing it. Instead, I believe it has everything to do with how and why we pursue what we pursue. My calling is deeply rooted in the truth that I was made to invite people to become the very best version of themselves possible.

I'm a people developer and I do this by inviting folks to consider things that might be both false or true about themselves as well as offering them tools that have proven to be helpful to me in my own growth and development and I can do that as a college professor, a business owner, a pastor, or a Mom.

Whatever we want to label it, our vocation, our calling, our "why," or our unique contribution, I think Buechner is exactly right. Gaining clarity on how I approach my work and my motivation for doing it, is forever tethered to the place inside me where my "deep gladness" joins up with a place or a people or a moment where the world has a "deep need." My only addition would be to make sure all this is happening in the place where we are meant to fit in, without someone tapping us on the shoulder saying, "Hey, I think you're in my spot."

Discovering our calling can feel big and mysterious and something only for mystics and theologians. I don't think it has to be that way. God knows all the answers to every question I've ever had about calling (and all the other things), I just keep forgetting to ask Him. In the very same chapter in Matthew, where Jesus teaches his disciples how to pray, and what fasting should look like, he talks to them about all the things they have worried about and will continue to stew over. It's not shocking to God that trying to figure out how to BE and DO in this life is cause for concern. As an answer to their worrying ways, Jesus just says, "Therefore I tell you, do not worry about your life…."

Currently, I'm in a season where I can find a lot to worry about and much of it is connected to my calling and contribution, I'm choosing to believe that this is an invitation to more faith. These days, rather than choosing what to do vocationally based on whether I would love doing it or not, I'm asking God to put me in the places he has for me and give me the wisdom and courage to follow Him there. If I can do that, I'm confident that my work, whatever it is, will be more a reflection of my willingness to be obedient rather than a defining of my identity or value.

TO CONSIDER

What lie have I believed about discovering and living out of my calling?

What truth could replace this lie?

What will knowing this truth change about the way I'm living?

Because change isn't a solo undertaking, who, among my trusted friends can I tell about this discovery?

Exhibit B: Help? Who needs help?

When I was five years old, I towered over my parents as they both lay waking up in their king-size bed. Hands on my hips, eyes big and wide, and a sassy attitude for days, I informed my mom and dad about what I would be wearing to school that day. For context, my mom had a rule about what was appropriate attire for school-aged girls. Four days a week, I had to wear a skirt or dress. One day a week, I could wear pants (remember, we're talking 1969 or so) and, to add insult to injury, my Brownie uniform counted as "pants wearing." That happened once a month, so there you go—I could wear pants to school a total of three times a month. I also want to go on the record and say that my brother had no such wardrobe limitations placed upon him. The injustice.

Back to the showdown in the bedroom—I was wearing pants for school that day, but I had already worn pants that week, and so Mom told me to go change my clothes. My five-year-old self wasn't having it. I jumped up onto their bed, stood between them, looking down at them. Definitely, I told them both (her mostly) that I WOULD be wearing pants again, because as every like-minded five-year-old would have declared, "I have my rights you know."

This story was told and retold my entire life, usually in the context of me saying something smart-alecky or argumentative. It was mostly used to reinforce a narrative of me as defiant, stubborn, or dramatic. For me, it has long been a picture of what I would experience over and over as a strong, confident, smart woman in the workplace. I believed, for decades, that to get my voice heard, I would need to be loud and demanding. I know now that this is just not true. Instead, I've learned that what I need to do to get my voice heard is to trust it. The more I learn to trust my own thoughts, ideas, and solutions the closer I get to stand to my authentic self—who I was always meant to be.

I think my parents admired my strength, even when they didn't really know how to direct it, like that day in their bedroom. I also believe they spent a lot of time worried that I would get in trouble because of it. My dad used to frequently tell me, after I would share a particularly energetic interaction I'd had with a boss or a co-worker, "You know, if you keep talking like that, you're going to get yourself fired." He always chuckled when he said it, so I think he admired my courage and yet was mildly terrified that I would get myself dismissed because of my mouth. It hasn't happened yet, in case you are wondering.

From the time I was little, even beyond giving my parents the business over wearing trousers instead of a skirt, I have been leading. And just so we're on the same page, I am defining leadership as anyone who has influence, anywhere.

I was the boss of the elementary school swing set. I was the self-assigned teacher, principal, and head coach of the "school" I ran for the neighborhood kids in the basement of my childhood home. I was a class officer and team captain in junior high and high school, and in college I found myself leading and directing whenever I got the chance—whether I was asked to or not.

I had a larger-than-life way about me. Part of it was natural gifting and part of it was an "I'm not sure where I actually belong so I'll be the loudest one in the room" stance. The leader inside of me was searching for a way to express herself. Sadly, at the time, and I am not sure much has changed, my coaches and teachers and professors and parents just didn't know what to do with all that energy I was bringing, nor did they know how to guide me in a healthy way of expressing it. On a side note, I'm pretty sure If I had been a boy, all my confidence would have been celebrated. Instead, I have been called loud, bossy, opinionated, and told that I have a big mouth my whole life. And trust me, it was not usually said as a compliment.

By the time I turned 40, I had been working and leading for over two decades and I was exhausted. I had held a host of jobs, worked in a variety of organizations, and was experiencing a particular kind of pattern in my leadership and work life. A group would get drawn to my energy and ideas, invite me to join the team, give me a space or a team to lead and then turn me loose—on my own. This is not a particularly good formula for me, and over the years has proven to be a bit of a set up for failure because I need people around me. I've learned I do better with a boss who coaches and guides and a team who supports and challenges. In the early years of leading, I'm confident I experienced leadership failures because I kept acting like I didn't need any help or guidance, in addition, part of it had to do with that loud, opinionated little girl hands on her hips demanding her rights.

Whatever the reason, after a while, everywhere I went, I would start to get bored and begin fantasizing about leaving. It started with criticizing the leadership, finding flaws in small things, and talking about how I would or could do it better.

What I know now is that I wasn't really bored or "better." Two things were happening, I was afraid and I had been given too much latitude in my leadership role, when what I needed was guidance and accountability. I needed someone who saw me for me, and wasn't overwhelmed or intimidated or worried. Someone who had done the work to discover his or her own leadership strengths, and weaknesses, and could invite me to do the same.

I have had only had three bosses do this for me in my nearly four decades of working, and I am forever grateful for the ways they each pushed past whatever it was about me that was getting in the way and kept inviting me to become a better version of me.

When I was in my early thirties, as I mentioned earlier, I stepped into the college classroom as an instructor for the first time. Of all the work I had done and enjoyed up to that point, nothing prepared me for the kind of joy and fulfillment being a college professor would bring me. For the first time, I experienced one of those "I was made for this" moments. It remains one of my favorite seasons of my professional life.

Unfortunately, every bright side seems to have a dark underbelly, and this was true for me in teaching. I got caught up in what I like to call the "classroom as kingdom" way of thinking. This approach is a set-up for folks like me. For men and women who have been trying to sort out their part, their place, their power base, the classroom can become like a micro-kingdom, and the one standing in the front holds all the power. I guess it wouldn't have to be just a classroom, it could be any room really—any place where you are the authority and there are no people to question or challenge you. Any time leaders are left unchecked, without accountability for what they are saying, how they are leading, and the ways this over-leveraged authority is leaking into the rest of their lives—well, that's not good. And it sure was not good for me.

Don't get me wrong, it felt good—every semester a new group of fresh-faced twenty-somethings would step into my little fiefdom, and I would get to be the one with all the knowledge and "rule" any old way I wanted. However, just for clarity's sake, I did not actually get to do whatever I wanted. I had a department chair who cared deeply about me, the university was accredited, and there were plenty of oversight committees—it just felt like I was ruling. And as I spent more years doing it, the more I liked it.

At the same time, as much as I enjoyed being in front of the classroom, I also cared deeply about my students, and some of them ended up being our house, dog, and babysitters. Many are still our friends today. I think I counted up one time and about a dozen students had a key to our house. I should probably think about getting those back someday.

Anyway, what was actually happening through my over-enjoyment of my self-imposed classroom power was having its deepest impact inside my heart and my head and it was really messing with my ego. I was starting to believe my own press, and that's rarely a good idea. Isn't that how it happens when leaders don't have the level of accountability they need? The first wave of harm comes into their own hearts and minds and lives first, at least that was true for me. I was disrespectful to my colleagues by missed meetings, I dishonored students by not taking the individual time he or she needed, I disregarded deadlines and failed to turn grades in on time, and I found myself "winging it" more and more in the classroom by not putting the time in for lecture prep like I knew I should.

Providentially, I did have the kind of accountability I needed. In time, the aforementioned department chair cared deeply about me and because she was paying attention, she saw me falling into the trap many young professors do—starting to hunger after students' approval more than making sure said students are learning what they are supposed to learn. She took me under her wing and taught me about what it meant to lead with humility, firmness, and grace in and out of the classroom, and she helped me get my grades turned in on time, too. It was the first time another leader did that for me and it changed me profoundly, inviting me to be a true leader in the classroom, which meant I needed to make room for both my true self and the students' hearts and minds. In his book, *The Courage to Teach*, Parker Palmer says it this way, "Face to face with my students, only one resource is at my immediate command: my identity, my selfhood, my sense of this "I" who teaches—without which I have no sense of the 'Thou' who learns."[3]

I was not very clear about my selfhood, let alone what students might need, in those early days of teaching. I had some natural gifting, a head for learning, and a heart for the learner, but I needed

> "Any time leaders are left unchecked, without accountability for what they are saying, how they are leading, and the ways this over-leveraged authority is leaking into the rest of their lives— well, that's not good. And it sure was not good for me."

guidance and a lot of it. Which meant, I needed to lean into my colleagues and my students much more than I was comfortable with. I asked my colleagues to look at my power-point or my lecture outlines to make sure they made sense and I was covering what I needed to cover. I shared with my Department Chair that I knew next to nothing about classroom management, other than being a mom of teenagers, and she got me set up with an effective online curriculum. With the students, I started blocking out more time for office hours so I could listen and respond to what gaps they were experiencing either in the learning or hands-on experiences and I stuck to my timetables —if I promised grades "by Friday," grades were done by Friday. In time, my classroom became less about what I wanted to get accomplished in a 50-minute session or an efficient transaction between teacher and student and more about creating opportunities to share knowledge and grow in wisdom and understanding of not only the content but the people who were learning it.

Teaching at the university brought me immense joy. It was a small, liberal arts, Christian college. I knew all of my colleagues and the majority of the students and they knew me. Our youngest was five-weeks-old when I started teaching and over time she would spend a big chunk of her pre-school days hanging out with me there. She became everybody's sweetheart. I got to have moments when I saw the lights of understanding go on for a student as he/she sorted out a particularly difficult concept. It was overall a sweet season. I felt for the first time, other than being a part of a consulting partnership, like I belonged. I was getting the opportunity to invest in the next generation and what I had to offer mattered. This near-decade of my professional life changed me in ways I, even today, have a difficult time articulating. A huge part of this change was acknowledging that the work both inside and outside the classroom could not be about me and I would need help to get that sorted out. A lot of help. Teaching was my "thing"; I felt it deep inside me that this is what I was made to do, but it couldn't just be about me. For it to matter in ways that went beyond what it did for me, I would have to learn that teaching that matters, as in something that gets exchanged and lasts longer than the next quiz or paper or final, would require an authentic and vulnerable offering. I would need to be willing to say, "I don't know," more frequently and ask my students to help the rest of us uncover and discover. As I grew in this vulnerable space, the learning became more of a shared experience among all of us, I became the guide, not the guru, and the students discovered they had more inside of them than they knew.

My father used to tell me to "Walk in like you own the place," whether I was walking onto the basketball court to play, onto the stage on opening night, or I was a grown woman starting a new job, that was his advice. It always made me think of that TV advertisement for deodorant, you know the one, "Don't ever let 'em see you sweat." The problem was, I DID NOT own the place and I was sweating—profusely. In all my years of living, I have been in plenty of situations where everything is all new and unknown, which brings with it a big wide open space where I could possibly fail or look foolish and when that happens, I get anxious. "Will they like me?" "Where will I sit?" " Who will I eat lunch with?" "Am I going to fit in?" In those moments, all I can see is my dad's face as he offered what I'm sure he thought was encouragement, but what I heard was "Don't be vulnerable or needy. Don't be the one who needs to ask for help." Everybody knows if you pretend you're fine, you're actually fine. Right?

When our youngest was a preschooler, she loved playing dress-up. We had a friend whose five daughters were in dance and we were the proud recipients of several years' worth of princess costumes multiplied by five. Yikes. It was a lot. During a particularly tough season for Mackenzie, I think her sister had started school full-time and she was lonely, she never wanted to take her pink princess dress off. "I a princess Mommy, I not Mackenzie," was her response when I would call her name and tell her to get some actual clothes on. It was more comforting for her to forget that she was just a normal four-year-old, with normal "problems" like nap times and absent siblings and instead, pretend to be someone else.

Pretty normal behavior for a big imagination-ed kiddo, but for me, after years and years of pretending, I wasn't nervous or flustered or acting as if I knew what I was doing when I clearly did not, I was struggling to remember who I actually was. I needed some help remembering. What my time at the university taught me was that it is OK to not know. And while they are helpful, my charisma, charm, and natural leadership gifting will only get me so far. I had to learn how to do the hard work of leading: to stay when everything in me wants to leave, to admit to not knowing when every fiber of my being wants to fake it, and with great gusto, to cheer others on and watch them thrive.

I used to believe that figuring it all out by myself would earn me a medal. Instead, for me, all this doing-it-on-my-own approach to working and leading has done is make me anxious, cause me to generate misunderstandings where they didn't need to be, and make me create unnecessary distance between myself and the team (students, employees, children, friends) and the problem we're trying to solve. This has been true everywhere I have had influence.

You know, if we're lucky and aware enough to realize it, before we pack up our desk for the last time, we'll figure out that there are things that matter and then there are things that really matter. The Bible explains the difference as some things being temporal (temporary) and some things being eternal (forever).

Whatever days I have left to lead, I want to focus on the latter. As in, I long to pour my heart into the eternal things. Because you know what? I have finished hundreds of projects over my years of working. Written dozens of sermons, graded too many papers to count, pulled together reports that nobody's reading anymore, and solved a couple of problems that created real change. I have also left enough places to know that few people will remember any of that, but what they will most definitely remember is the way they felt about themselves when we were together. Did they know that I was really listening, were they confident that their story mattered to me, did they know for sure I saw them for who they actually were and invited them to become more of that? Or, did they think I was faking it?

Gosh, I hope not. I hope people are left with the memory of me being fully present with them. Because that's where the eternal things live—in the way our hearts swell when someone acknowledges our gifting and asks for more, in that instant where our imagination unlocks to what might be because someone believes in us, and in that spark of a moment where a dream becomes reality because a leader said, "Go for it."

I left the university after nearly a decade. It was one of the most difficult endings of my professional life, but what I took with me was my own sort of master class of learning in leadership. I'm still tempted to worry about pleasing the boss or the team over producing good work, and to believe the only person I can trust is myself. But I'm learning, and sometimes the greatest leadership move I make is to lead myself right into taking my hands off my hips, lowering my voice, and honestly asking for the help I need and offering it where it makes sense.

TO CONSIDER

What lie have I believed about my own need for help when leading (wherever that might be) and how it might be helping or hurting me?

What truth could replace this lie?

What will knowing this truth change about the way I'm living?

Because change isn't a solo undertaking, who, among my trusted friends can I tell about this discovery?

EXHIBIT C: MOVING ON IS NOT QUITTING

Sometimes you just have to leave. Quit. Fire yourself. Retire. Take a break. I'm not sure what it needs to be called in your life, but for me, I've had to "move on" many, many times. For years I thought I was failing in some way. I kept hearing my Dad's voice in my head, "Settle down, find something to do that you love and it won't feel like work at all." That just hasn't been my experience. I have found so many "somethings to do" and have loved parts of all of them, but they have also, at times, felt like a lot of difficult and hard work and that's OK.

I was raised by a dad who worked in the same field (education) for his entire professional life. My mom was primarily a stay at home mom and while she did have a couple part-time jobs outside the home, her full-time gig was us, her three children (which trust me, was plenty of work).

So, my ideas about work, professional life, and "career" came from watching my dad navigate his. Dad started as a teacher/coach, got his Master's Degree in teaching, his certification in administration and became a high school principal. After a couple of years at that, he went back to school and got his Doctorate in Education, and focused on Secondary Education, which enabled him to become an assistant superintendent in the second largest school system in our state—he was 38 years old. Dad was focused and accomplished and goal driven when it came to his career (and lots of other things too). He loved education and wanted to make a difference in the field he was passionate about.

My siblings exhibited that same clear-mindedness about their careers as well. My older sister wanted to be a teacher and became one, passionately and successfully teaching kindergarten and/or first grade for 39 years (she just retired; I'm jealous). My brother talked about being a veterinarian from the time he was in middle school and is now in his 34th year of practicing. He owns his own thriving practice and is beloved by his clients and all of us in the family, especially those of us who have animals. (I mean come on, do you know how expensive it is to have an animal these days?)

I have always admired my dad's tenacity and focus as well as my siblings', but never quite shared the career clarity or the passion for any one thing. I would be less than honest if I didn't tell you that sometimes I wondered what was wrong with me—why couldn't I find my "thing" (see the chapter Calling)?

I went to college and majored in Marketing and Management and as I've already shared, I've had a lot of jobs. I got a job in a clothing store and became the assistant manager. We moved and I began working for one of my former professors in his consulting firm. I moved from that and went to work for a publishing company where I was a writer and the director of Marketing Research. We moved again when I was pregnant with a 7-month-old at home. So I left publishing and was a contractor for another consulting firm. That firm went under and so my friend and I hung out our own shingle and started doing some consulting on our own. We moved again and I was asked to teach a class as an adjunct at a local Christian university. I went back to school, got my Master's Degree in Communications, and became an Associate Professor at that university. After a season, I felt called into ministry and joined the staff of the church my family was attending at the time. I left full-time church work, went back to consulting, and stepped into running an internship program for a local organization. I left the internship leadership role and took on the role of Chief Culture Officer at a bank. A few months ago, I left that role and find myself once again consulting.

My dad and I talked a lot about all my changes. One of the things I so appreciated was even though he was a pretty singularly focused guy when it came to work, he was supportive of me and my journey of ever-changing roles. I'm sure he and Mom were worried at times and we did have some, "Are you sure you know what you're doing?" conversations when I would announce yet another transition. However, never once did Dad shame me or make me feel "less than" because of all the job jumps.

I am not, by nature, a restless person (even though all those ca-reer changes might indicate otherwise), so the moves weren't due to that. Rather, each transition has been connected to a sense of God inviting me to trust him as we move together into "next." There have been seasons when I was more deeply aware of that invitation than others, but whether I was a business consultant, a stay at home mom, a college professor, a pastor, or a retail manager, the passing on to the next assignment has been a step of faith—going somewhere I've never been before—and it has been a little scary. OK, that's not quite true—it's been A LOT scary. Recently, I had a much respected boss say to me, "Suze, you're a traveler when it comes to work and travel-ers move on when it's time." That statement helped me put the right words to something I've long struggled with in these transitions; I'm not abandoning or quitting (which is how I've sometimes felt), I'm traveling.

When I arrived at my last assignment, a bank, I came with two other colleagues who were also friends. None of the three of us knew anything about banking, other than the fact that a bank was where your paycheck went every two weeks and bankers are the people who may, or may not, loan you money when you need it. We weren't there to be bankers; we were there to take care of and provide growth opportunities for those who were bankers. It was an exciting move, one filled with lots of possibilities for inviting folks to explore and become more of who they were always meant to be. However, within 10 months of our arrival our team changed as our leader un-expectedly left and I stepped into the role of team lead. A few months after that, we were faced with the task of keeping the staff informed and safe in the midst of a worldwide pandemic. In the midst of year one of the pandemic protocols, the president of the organization an-nounced his resignation, and then at the end of that year my remain-ing teammate got engaged and let me know she would be leaving as well. In the summer of 2021, a new President came on board and gave the team a much needed jumpstart back toward growth. Need-less to say, a lot changed in a short amount of time.

Our team had come to the bank to pour into team members

through training and development. All that changed with the people and leadership transitions as well as COVID-19. The organization was growing, but not quite big enough to support my role. So, just three years into the journey, I found myself alone and kind of directionless, which is a pretty dangerous place for my emotional and physical well-being. I was serving alongside people I cared deeply about, but I didn't have a clear sense of why anymore. I'm grateful to say, I had people to process this with—my husband, my good friend, Maddie (the one who got married and left), and the president of the bank. Without telling me what to do, each of these wise and loving folks helped me see what was right in front of my face—it was time to go. Again.

Leaving any place, and the people who make up that place, you care about is difficult. Actually, I've also found that leaving a place you don't care about can be difficult too. After all, if the job (or neighborhood, or house, or town, or school) didn't hold any relational connection for me, if I hadn't found people to meaningfully share pieces and parts of this 40-50 hour per week segment of my life with—what was the point? There are always going to be things to DO, but the best part of working for me has always been the people I get to do it with.

I have long thought, and then over the years came to believe, that it would be horrible to leave a place, or say good-bye to anyone I had shared work time and space with, and have it not matter. Whether we're somewhere for three years or 30, it should matter that we were there. There should be shared stories and laughter and successes and failures—work is rarely a solitary adventure (even if you work for yourself or by yourself). It's been my experience that if the work matters to me and if the people I'm doing this work with have provided any big, or small, level of connection, it will be tough to leave.

I'm a crier and I have shed tears of joy when leaving somewhere, and I have wept buckets because of a broken heart over the leaving—both were important. For good or for ill, I think Mother Teresa was right when she said, "People will forget the things you do, and people will forget the things you say. But people will never forget how you made them feel." I've forgotten a lot of things over the years—but I could tell you exactly how I felt with every boss, place, and team I've ever left.

I'm convinced, and this is not rocket science, that there's a beginning, a middle and an end to everything. Relationships, seasons, crises, and careers—all of them have a starting place, a middle ground, and an ending. The $24,000 question is: how do you know where you are in that process?

The beginning is pretty easy to identify, but how long do you get to stay there? The middle years (or months sometimes) can be the season that happens to you without you really knowing it. You're just remaining faithful, doing the work, getting the projects finished and before you know it you've been somewhere 5, 10, 20 years. It's the ending for me, how does one know when it's time to go? How do you know the difference between bringing closure to your contribution and saying good-bye or just out-an-out giving up?

I worked at a church for nearly a dozen years. All of my 40s were spent there, doing work I felt called to do, alongside so many people I came to love deeply. My faith deepened and my calling got clarity because of my time there. I was challenged and welcomed and it became the season of my life I always think of as the most transformative—both personally and professionally. The work and the place were such good fits for me, until they weren't. In the fall of 2016 I began what would become the "ending" season there—I just didn't know it at the time. For months, after I clearly heard God tell me that my time there was coming to a close, I tried to keep myself in the "middle" years. Maybe, I thought, if I did a different job or worked on a different team in the church I could remain? When you work at a church, it becomes both your workplace tribe and your faith community. There were, and still are, people there I cared about deeply and it's difficult to leave when the people matter as much as those folks mattered to me. Plus, I hate change. I hate starting over, learning new systems, processes, and personalities. The older I get, the more my dislike for it grows. Over time, God kept nudging me toward departure. Sometimes the guidance was painful and lonely, but it was always loving. In the spring of 2017 I knew—all my stalling tactics were just that, activities I was making up so I could stay a little longer.

I've thought alot about the seven months it took me to yield to the Godly prompting to leave. I've processed a lot of the conversations, the silence, the tears, the misunderstandings, and the difficulty I had in letting go. At times it felt like I was being asked to entrust a beloved piece of art to someone who might come in with new paint and brushes to radically change it, which seemed wrong in so many ways. At other times it felt like I couldn't get out of there fast enough.

> "Whether we're somewhere for three years or 30, it should matter that we were there. There should be shared stories and laughter and successes and failures..."

Mark Twain said that the only people who like change are babies with wet diapers—clearly, he never tried to hold down a squirming baby and change a very dirty diaper. Honestly, I don't think anybody, even the people who proclaim loudly, "I love change," really finds a deep and abiding joy in change. It can be fun to move the furniture around, it can feel like an adventure to sell the house and buy the RV and travel the country (no experience on that one), it can even sound exciting to leave a job without another one to jump into (too much experience here). Even amidst the upbeat energy that change can bring, our humanity remains. We're wired for rhythms and predictable patterns—sleep, wake, eat, activity, eat, activity, eat, activity, sleep, start over—and when those structures get scrambled by change, it might take us a little bit to find our healthy footing again.

Personally, there have been buckets and buckets of change over the last five years—the last kid graduated from high school, I transitioned out of not one but three jobs, we moved, we left our church, found a new church, learned how to work and live differently due to a worldwide pandemic, and both of my parents passed away. I'm change-weary. That weariness and the need to constantly embrace a "new normal" has me thinking that one of the reasons I've begun to resist change is my nagging worry that the next transition will be the one where I don't find my equilibrium again and I'm set adrift. In all the transitions and moves and leaps, that's never happened. Yet, I'm still fearful that this time might be the time.

I don't think that's true. I'm in the middle of a transition now, as I write these words, and while I have moments of thinking "what in the world have I done?" and "how in the heck are we gonna pay the bills?," I have more moments when I know, without an inkling of a doubt, that I will find my way once again. There will be good work for me to do and amazing people for me to do it with.

Back when she was trying to figure out whether it was time to leave the bank or not, my friend, Maddie was wrestling with that age old question, "Should I stay or should I go?" and her then fiance (now husband) told her, "You know, moving on isn't quitting—it's just... moving on." Thanks Jake, that phrase has come back to me over and over, holding my hand as I have made tough decisions about moving on or staying put and it's helped me leave with all of my "me-ness" intact. Because as much as it wants to, work just doesn't get to define me anymore.

TO CONSIDER

What lie have I believed about a transition choice I'm faced with right now? What would it mean if I stayed? What would it mean if I moved on?

What truth could replace this lie?

What will knowing this truth change about the way I'm living?

Because change isn't a solo undertaking, who, among my trusted friends can I tell about this discovery?

PART 5: EMOTIONS

LIE
Your feelings can't be trusted.

TRUTH
Your emotions are a gift from the One who made you. Like an indicator light on the dashboard of your car, they are there to serve you. Trust yourself—and your emotions.

Emotions are an enormous part of our lives. Even people who say they aren't "emotional" have deep feelings about things and people and events, they just may not ever let those emotions out. I'm convinced that emotions are a gift, given to serve us but not to have mastery over us. I'm a "lead from my heart" kind of person (as in I should never play poker) and yet, I grew up believing my emotions couldn't be trusted. I've been asked to "Tone it down," "Stop being so dramatic," and I have repeatedly been told, "That's why women shouldn't lead," for more years than I'd like to count...

Today, I believe the part of me that is my emotional tool box is just that—tools to help me navigate life. I DO have big feelings, but I understand now that these emotions are a gift from the One who made me. Learning to identify WHAT I'm feeling and learning to determine HOW that feeling is supposed to help me is a life-long adventure. It's taken me a significant amount of time and a large chunk of change spent on therapy to begin to understand that emotions are important and serve a really important purpose in my life. This may be a shock to some, there are more than three emotions (fear, shame, anger) and the evidence presented in this section explores how we might learn to trust emotions and let them do their job in our lives. This exploration is a journey and not a journey to take alone.

> *"Vulnerability is the birthplace of love, belonging, joy, courage, empathy, and creativity. It is the source of hope, empathy, accountability, and authenticity. If we want greater clarity in our purpose or deeper and more meaningful spiritual lives, vulnerability is the path."*
>
> BRENÉ BROWN[1]

EXHIBIT A: WE ALL HAVE
THEM FOR A REASON

What is it with emotions, and what seems to be the human being's very complicated relationship with them? As far as I can tell, we seem to fall into one of two camps: we either believe that emotions are necessary and add good "stuff" to our lives or, emotions are dumb and a waste of time. There's probably a more scientific way to articulate that—but since I'm not a scientist, I'll say that my response to both of those statements is "agreed." Emotions are necessary and good in addition to being really complicated and time consuming to understand.

For as long as I can remember, I have had deep access to my emotions. I have very clear memories of feeling lots of things: happiness, sadness, joy, fear, belonging, love, and loneliness to name a few. I wasn't raised by traditionally "emotional" people, as in I didn't observe my parents expressing their emotions much. For example, when I was diagnosed with Cancer as a 15 year old, I have no memory of my parents crying about or pounding their fist on the table at the injustice of their otherwise healthy teenage daughter being diagnosed with a life-threatening disease. Much later, when I had kids of my own and one of my fears was one of them getting sick, I asked my parents about their seeming stoicism and their response was something like, "Oh, there were plenty of tears and anger and begging God to make it better, we just didn't do that in front of you." This unwillingness to share what they were feeling about me, with me, caused all kinds of confusion about how much they cared and their thoughts about the words "your daughter" and "has Cancer" in the same sentence. I had so many emotions about it all. I felt angry that this was happening to me when it was happening. I was confused by all the medical talk and all the doctors and the many procedures. I was hurt when people didn't understand or want to understand everything that was happening. I was profoundly disappointed by the many things like sports, the spring play, and time with friends I was missing out on. I felt scared. A lot. I would retreat to my room where I could play out my worst fears and then worry about them all by myself. Even though there always seemed to be people around, I felt alone and isolated most of the time. Meanwhile, from what I could see and perceive, my parents were feeling very little.

Of course, I understand now, my parents' emotions must have been all over the place after receiving the news of my diagnosis, but they made the best decision they could make at the time about how to process that news. I discovered much later, their decision to not talk to me about their feelings or mine was made from a place of love and protection. They were trying to keep me from more pain. I get it, and yet...that choice to remain silent with me about their questions and concerns and fear, let alone mine, did cause me pain. All that time in my room speculating about whether I would live to be sixteen, get my drivers license, maybe a boyfriend, and go to college, ended up generating a lot of shame about my sometimes paralyzing fear. I remember thinking, "Why can't I hold it all together like Mom and Dad" and all the while they weren't holding it together at all—they were faking it.

Isn't that the way it is sometimes? We find ourselves in an incredibly difficult situation, something we've never been through before, and end up in a misunderstanding with people we care deeply about. Everyone's just doing the best with what they know, and sometimes that best is misunderstood or might even cause harm, either to ourselves or the other person. Rarely is that harm because we intended for our communication or response to be hurtful, but because there is often a kind of agonizing spillover of pain when life goes topsy-turvy.

This experience and a few others, caused me to believe a lie that would be a part of my operating system for a very long time: my feelings were too much and they could not be trusted.

For years, in the study of a human's emotional make-up, psychologists reported that any given person experienced six basic emotions: happiness, sadness, anger, surprise, fear, and disgust.[2] The thinking was that every other spin-off emotion, like joy and grief, would find its roots in one of these six. Then, in 2014 a group of researchers from UC Berkely published an article that said humans actually experience 27 basic emotions, expanding the list to include things like admiration, adoration, aesthetic appreciation, amusement, anxiety, awe, awkwardness, boredom, calmness, confusion, contempt, craving, disappointment, empathic pain, entrancement, envy, excitement, guilt, horror, interest, joy, nostalgia, pride, relief, romance, satisfaction, sexual desire, sympathy, and triumph.[3] However short or long the list, my thought is that our emotional state of being is both fascinating and incredibly difficult to pin down. This complexity may be part of the reason some people work really hard to detach from their emotional selves and the reality that is theirs because of emotions.

A long time ago, someone much older and wiser told me to think about my emotions like servants rather than a master—there to help me, not to enslave me. I've thought about that often. When I'm fearful, instead of giving in to the fear and spiraling into thought patterns difficult for me to get out of, what if I first tried to determine what I was actually afraid of? With the real fear identified, I could then ask myself how that fear might help me as I keep moving forward with life. Trust me, I frequently forget to ask myself those questions and get sucked into the black hole that is worst case scenario thinking. It often takes the husband asking me, "What movie is playing in your head right now?" to get me to snap out of it and lay the fear (or sadness or anxiety or pride or envy) down, so life can go on.

I actually believe my emotions, in all their nuanced and complex forms, are a gift. Tools given to me by the One who made me so I can navigate my life in a way that holds all the richness that living life has to offer me. Is it complicated? You bet. Unlike facts and data, emotions hold the potential for misunderstanding, confusion, and relational fractures. Wouldn't life be boring if all we had to build a life with was certainty?

To feel things deeply, I think, is a particular kind of grace. To know what to do with those feelings...well, that's a skill. And like any competency you want to get better at, practicing real life application of my emotions has taken time and intention. I have always had the feelings but I haven't always known what they should be telling me or how I should even respond to them. I've experienced fear, sadness, joy, exhilaration, apathy, frustration, peace, and lots more. I've also had to learn how to listen to those feelings and then think through what they are trying to tell me or how they might serve me? That has been a difficult journey inward.

Two things happened that launched me on this quest. The first thing I started paying attention to was a growing weariness inside me that grew out of hearing people say things to me like, "Once you stop being so emotional about it, you'll be able to understand what I'm trying to say," or some other equally diminishing phrase. The second "event" was when I hit a point in my life when I knew I had to stop just observing my emotional life, as in just speaking to the air or writing in my journal, "I feel lonely." It was time for me to start participating in my emotional life and do the work required to discover why I might be lonely, or sad or scared or a variety of other things. The decision to fully participate changed my relationship with my emotional well-being; it has also taken time, a commitment to learning, a willingness to be humble, and remaining open to accountability.

In order to fully understand the "why" behind any particular emotion I might be feeling, I had to learn how to find my way back to the origin of the thing. I had to discover, learn, practice, and then own my emotional health. There was a whole big season of my life when this was what I focused on. I did this with the help of a trusted counselor, as a part of the discipling relationship already shared in an earlier chapter, I learned more about my personality, and I had regular time alone with my Bible and my journal. I began to explore questions I had been wrestling with for a long time. Were my emotions just bubbling up inside of me all the time with no start or finish, or was there some kind of pattern to them, some way to predict a feeling or a response? Before I even started to dive into that, I had to wrestle through a lot of shame, which is my "go to" emotion, about what I was sure was my late arrival to the emotional intelligence learning curve. When I looked around me, it seemed like all the other adults in my life weren't worrying like I was or getting their feelings hurt with the frequency I experienced, or even feeling as hopeful as I did at times. This season of intentional focus on my emotional health helped me see that I wasn't alone on the adventure of discovery. Instead, with the simple act of taking my eyes off myself, I could see that mostly every other human I knew was on the same journey, just in a different place.

Way smarter people than me have studied, researched, tested, and written about the relationship between our thoughts, feelings, and behavior. What is controlling what? Are our thoughts in charge or our emotions, and then, what about our actions? How does it all fit together and why do I even care?

For me, in order to grow in my personal emotional understanding, I've actually had to come to the realization that my heart is my default. I feel first, think second, and act third. Like the engine in my car, the way I feel about something is powering how I think about it, and those thoughts then guide how I act. So, when my emotional responses seem to be more calibrated, and my thinking is clear, the way I behave is a bit more thoughtful and dependable. For instance, when I get an unexpected text from someone saying they were thinking about me, it makes me feel grateful, and my thoughts tend to be positive toward that person, and then I will most likely respond back with kindness. However, if I feel rejected by someone, I might tend to think I've been slighted by that person, and my default setting would be to pull back, both physically and emotionally, from that person. It seems like it has taken me years to fully understand and trust that it is my heart that is leading and that's OK. My emotions, even when they're complicated or big, can be trusted.

We all have a default response when it comes to how we emotionally respond to highly, or even marginally, charged situations—we either think, feel, or do first. Maybe like me, your heart wants to lead the way and you have to drag your thinking and your action along for the ride. Or maybe you're more like my husband, whose thinking tends to lead the way and then he has to be intentional about not letting his heart and body fall too far behind. Possibly, you're more like my good friend Allyson who moves to action quickly but has trained her heart and head to follow almost as quickly. Whatever that default is, I just want to say that I've learned I need all three—feeling, thinking, and doing—if I'm going to live a life that feels relatively balanced. Which in the end, is better for me and everyone else around me.

When I was 27 years old something profoundly painful happened to me. Kelly and I had been married for a little over five years at that point and we had yet to bring any babies into our little tribe, so it was just the two of us and the dog. We were mostly doing well. However, there was a bit of a sticky place: my relationship with my father-in-law was not as easy as I longed for it to be. Sometimes this made sense to me because Kelly was trying to navigate his own tumultuous relationship with his Dad and I found myself, in the early married years, following his lead. Later in our marriage, I was just longing for some kind of meaningful relationship with my father-in-law, but it was always just out of reach.

In the first couple years of our marriage, we lived just five minutes from Kelly's folks, so we were frequently together. One evening we were at the in-laws' house for dinner, and afterward we were talking. As the conversation progressed, it was evident that the FIL and I were standing on different sides of the topic, which was pretty normal for us. After a few back and forths, my husband's father got silent, looked me square in the eye and said he was done debating because, "You know Suze I've never really liked you anyway."

Shock.

Hurt.

Pain.

Anger.

Rejected.

Shame.

Royally pissed off.

Unloved.

These are a few of the things I was feeling at that moment and as

I looked across the room at Kelly, and he gathered us both up and we left, I made a decision about my father-in-law. That man was never going to receive my affection again. I would build a wall between us so he could not hurt me like that again and I did it for 23 years.

FEELINGS drive THOUGHTS which guide ACTIONS.

I held that emotional wall in place all those years because in my mind I was justified. Every time I would think something was improving between us, he would say something or do something that I perceived as mean or controlling, and it all went back to that evening in their living room when he declared his dislike of me. Time after time, the barrier between us was reinforced.

"That's what unforgiveness does—it keeps the one holding on to the pain captive."

This continued until he fell in their home and suffered a traumatic brain injury and it quickly became clear he may never return to his normal active self, let alone survive. Because, don't forget, our brains are in charge of so much more than our emotions. At the time of the fall, Kelly's folks were living in Oklahoma. So, for the nine weeks that remained of his Dad's life, Kelly and his sister shared the "being with" responsibility. One of those weeks, when Kelly was in Oklahoma, I had a dream. In the dream, I saw myself leaning over my father-in-law, praying with him and giving him a kiss—on the mouth. My first thought when I woke up was, "Ummm..no way in hell that is happening," and then I prayed.

As I prayed, I sensed the Lord inviting me to tear that wall between Phil and I down. Time was growing short for Phil and it was entirely too short to hold on to a 23-year-old hurt. So, I asked God to do what only the Divine can do in those situations; help me see what was happening that night when I felt so deeply wounded by this man, God's beloved son, who now lay dying. God's kind like that. When we ask Him to help us see, He mostly always does. In prayer,

I asked the Lord to take me back to that night and in so doing, I had an image of Jesus standing behind Phil as he sat in his recliner and launched those hurtful words my way. Jesus was not just standing behind Phil, He had his hands gently on his shoulders and as I gazed upon that scene, I sensed in my spirit Jesus saying to me, "Suze, he doesn't know what he's doing or why he's saying this." At that moment, it all fell away. All the years of hurt and keeping score and protecting myself and my family. I was able to ask for forgiveness for my decades of grudge-keeping. Then I was able to forgive Phil. It took me a lot of energy to stay behind that wall for all those years and honestly, probably caused me the most hurt. Uugh, that's what unforgiveness does—it keeps the one holding on to the pain captive. I do wish I had gotten there sooner, but regret isn't helpful or life giving and so I moved on. Soon after that prayer time, Kelly called and told me to pull the kids out of school and come, his Dad didn't have long. We jumped in the car to head west, and when we got there we held my mother-in-law close and helped Phil make the transition to hospice. When it came time to get back in the car and head East, so the kids could get back to school and work, I went into Phil's room to say good-bye. I knew this was the last time we would be together on this side of heaven. I also knew there was not a wall between us anymore. As I leaned over his bed, I told him, "Thank you." Thank you for Kelly, for all his generosity over the years, and for sharing his love of music with me. He looked at me like he knew me, which I wasn't sure of after suffering a Traumatic Brain Injury, and began to sing This Little Light of Mine. I joined him and when we finished, I put my hand on his arm, told him I loved him, leaned down and kissed him right on the mouth. Not because of the dream, but because I meant it, all of it.

All those years of thinking, feeling, and doing a particular way with Phil were gone. It doesn't mean the pain wasn't real and if I think about it too long, I can conjure up a lot of the crappy stuff that happened between us over 20 plus years. But I don't do that anymore. Mostly, when I do think about my father-in-law, it's in light of his brokenness that led him to unkindness. When I do that, I find pieces and parts of my own story looking right back at me and the forgiveness remains—steadfast and steady and safe. And the only emotion I can access is love.

TO CONSIDER

What lie have I believed about my emotions (too many, too little?) and the role they should play in the living of my life?

What truth could replace this lie?

What will knowing this truth change about the way I'm living?

Because change isn't a solo undertaking, who, among my trusted friends can I tell about this discovery?

Exhibit B: The Big Three

I've done some reflecting backward and, as near as I can figure, I don't think I was ever bullied. I remember people telling me I had a big mouth (I did) and I couldn't keep a secret (I couldn't), but I don't have any memories in this cobweb of a brain of mine that lead me to believe I was ongoingly intimidated by another either verbally, emotionally, or physically, and for that, I'm grateful. I am, however, very clear that I have been bullied in a sense by my own particular collection of emotions.

The National Center Against Bullying defines a bully's activities as, "An ongoing and deliberate misuse of power in relationships through repeated verbal, physical and/or social behavior that intends to cause physical, social and/or psychological harm."[4] If that's the case, then I would say some of my bigger emotions like anger, shame, and fear have definitely been bullies in my life. Like a giant standing in the shadows, these three have loomed large at times and intimidated me into not feeling what it was I was actually meant to feel.

I have been driving a Volkswagen convertible for the past 15 years and gosh, do I love that little car. I've had two, one gray and one black (boring, I know), and tooling around town with the lid down on a warm summer night, on the way to get ice cream, is pretty close to perfect for me. Lots of people have commented over the years, as they sit beside me at a stoplight, about how much fun the car must be to drive. I used to tell Kelly, "Driving this car is like free therapy," until he reminded me that we had a car payment—so there's that. All that to say, as shallow as it sounds, having a convertible has brought me a lot of joy over the years. I feel safe behind the wheel, not just in a "standards of safety" way, but like a sheltering kind of way. Anyway, one night early in the summer I was coming home from a friend's house with the lid down, music blasting, and I was in that cocoon of happiness. Without even being aware I was doing it, I drifted a bit into the lane next to me. Out of nowhere, there was rage being launched my way by the driver of the pick-up truck I had nearly cut off. As I recall, there was pounding on the side of her car, flipping me off, and more than one F-bomb being hurled into the night sky. Honestly, I was scared. She pulled in front of me and slowed down, forcing me to do the same and all I could feel was fear. Big, anxiety inducing fear. My heart was racing, my stomach was in my throat, and for the life of me it felt like my brain was off-line. All I could think was that she was going to pull a gun out and point it at me and here I was in this dinky convertible with the lid down.

Well, there were no pistols pulled and eventually she sped off. As I sat at a stoplight, I started crying. I pulled into the closest parking lot, put the car in park, and tried to figure out what in the world was happening. I couldn't stop shaking and crying, even though the "danger" had passed.

That's what I mean by some of our emotions being bullies. The fear I felt in the moment was justified, but the way it kept hanging around kept me from sorting out what I was actually feeling and it seemed too big for the incident. I took a few deep breaths, closed my eyes and offered a prayer of thanksgiving (for that non-existent firearm), and started driving again. As I made my way home, I realized that with the fear out of the way, I could feel what seemed like a violation of sorts—all that rage directed at me, while I was in my "safe" place. I was embarrassed, in a weird way, that someone I will never see again, would think I was an irresponsible driver. Later, as I talked about it with Kelly, I also realized I had a certain sense of sadness that this is who a big part of our culture is now—angry, frustrated, violent, and probably scared themselves.

I'm convinced that we all have an emotional "bully" of some kind or another. Maybe it's anger when you get interrupted or corrected, or shame when you start comparing something of yours with someone else's. It may not be fear when you get yelled at in traffic, but it's there and because it is, it's important to have the tools in our emotional toolbox to push past whatever those big, bully-like emotions are and find out what's really going on. Because when we figure out what's truly behind that "bully," we can keep moving forward into the big, beautiful life that's been planned for us.

For me, the greatest tool I have when I'm feeling some of those big emotions, is to pause and ask myself, "What is making you mad, sad, or glad?"

This question, right behind, "Will you marry me," has been the most important question anyone ever asked me. I'm not kidding. It might seem simplistic or childlike to some, but for me it was like a flashlight clicking on in a darkened room. I would say that I am someone who is pretty self aware, and more than marginally connected to my emotional center. Yet, I haven't always known what to do with all the emotions I'm experiencing or noticing. This question became my guide in a way, helping me look underneath the surface of those big emotions and find out what was really going on. Our motivation behind something is always more authentically revealing than our behavior because of something. Like a toddler who behaves badly when they don't get the sugary cereal at the grocery store, their motivation is most likely not that he woke up that morning and thought, "I'm going to get Mom to buy me Lucky Charms today." Most likely, the toddler tantrum set in because of sleepiness or hunger or some other mysterious pre-school motivator. Motivation eclipses behavior, every time and the more I know about what motivates me, the greater chance I have of saying on the journey of becoming the best version of me possible.

So, with help, I began to explore this "mad, sad, glad" thing. I began to pay attention when something in my exterior world triggered an emotion like frustration, betrayal, or joy. Instead of just "going with it," I began to try and take a moment to observe what was actually happening—no judgment, just the facts. After taking a beat for some fact-finding, I would try and discern why all of "that" (whatever was happening at the time) was making me feel what I was feeling.

For instance, my husband likes to use a lot of details to tell me a story. I'm more of a "bottom line" kind of gal. So, sometimes, when he gets going on a story, I can get pretty frustrated. If I don't pay attention to that feeling, and ask "why" it's happening, I can end up angrily cutting Kelly's story off and asking him to "just get to the point already." Trust me, it happens. A lot.

Instead, if I take a beat when I notice the emotion rising, ask myself what might be actually going on, I usually can get to an answer pretty quickly. Maybe I'm late for an appointment or I was in the middle of a thought myself —most often I discovered I wasn't angry at all. I was sometimes actually frustrated, worried, afraid, anxious, or maybe even feeling mistreated.

With enough practice, you can begin to catch yourself in real time, before you behave badly or inappropriately, and discover what's truly motivating the emotions you're feeling. Many times, after uncovering my "true" emotion and what's driving it, I often discovered that the thing I thought was making me mad, sad, or glad was somehow connected to a lie I believed. In order to not get stuck there again, because lies can be like cement blocks around our feet and keep us from growing, I've learned I need to change my mind about that lie and start to believe something truer. New beliefs often require an assist. For me, because I'm a Jesus girl, that means I need to spend time with God asking what in the world He is trying to say to me in all this. That inquiry is most effective when it's followed up with another God directed question, "What should I do next, so when this happens again, I'm different?" Because that's the goal—it's not to not get mad anymore (that's not even a thing), or not to feel any sadness or grief, or even to not to be joyful and celebrate when that's what is called for. Rather, the goal is to learn to catch ourselves as we're feeling our feelings, recognizing that whatever emotion we are contending with might just be trying to show us something we've been believing that's just not true. If I can identify that lie and replace it with the truth, I might begin to experience what it means to live a transformed life.

For 26 years we have lived in Fort Wayne, IN. For the first 23 of those years we were situated in an older part of town where the garages were detached and there was a lot of parking in the street. This was especially helpful when you're teaching 15 year olds how to parallel park. Right around the corner from our house was a candy shop, a drug store, a gas station and a couple of bars. In the spring of 2012, at 5 a.m., a drunk driver came flying down our street and smashed into and totaled two of our three cars. After wading through all the police reports and insurance and rental cars, we had two cars to look for and purchase. The husband and I decided that he would do the tracking down of cars and I would take care of the financial details; it felt like a good division of labor. However, as time went on and neither one of our cars was being replaced, I found myself getting really angry at Kelly. I remember thinking I had done my part, all financing for the purchases was pre-approved and ready to go, why hadn't he held up his end of the bargain and found the cars we were going to buy? Gratefully, I had already been taught the "mad, sad, glad" tool and before my anger and frustration turned toward Kelly like an accusatory laser, I did the work required and started looking underneath the water line as to what was actually going on.

I paid attention to the facts: we needed to replace those cars, Kelly said he would do it, he wasn't doing it, we needed to return the loaners to the people who had been so generous, the financing for the purchases was in place, I had done my part. I was irritated and angry.

After making a laundry list of the facts, I then did some reflecting on why any or all the things I had listed mattered: Kelly made a promise and he didn't keep it. We were inconveniencing the folks who had loaned us the cars and I had some embarrassment about that. I was tired of sharing the one remaining car (which was mine). I felt like this was a pattern with us when it came to big decisions: I have to do it or it won't get done. We were getting ready for a kid to go to college, how were we going to afford two additional car payments? I felt disrespected by Kelly. I wasn't actually angry after all, I was hurt, disappointed, embarrassed, and afraid.

After completing those two steps on my own, the "what" and the "why," I talked to Kelly about all of what I was feeling and why. It ended up being super helpful. He was able to own the fact that he hadn't tracked down any cars because he was overwhelmed and didn't want to ask for help. I was able to ask for forgiveness for the ways I had been silently judging him and not so silently taking out my fear and shame and hurt on him. We came up with a good plan for moving forward and once again, what could have divided us didn't have its way and we were a team again.

I still had some work to do though. I asked God what it was He was trying to tell me through all of this...and the response I sensed inside my heart was that He wanted me to know that He was not going to abandon me when life got complicated and I wasn't going to have to figure it all out by myself. I then had to ask the second, very important question, "God, what should I do the next time this happens?" and His response was one that seems simple in the receiving but is so difficult in the living; "Trust me."

I had to get practical though, because I knew it would happen again—something wouldn't go according to my plan and I would get hurt, afraid, embarrassed, or some other emotion. So, the plan I came up with, which seems to go with God's words of trust, was, the next time I felt myself going to that place of, "Fine, I guess I'll have to do it all by myself," I needed to stop and ask myself if that was actually true. Whether it was or wasn't, I then needed to ask for help. I had to practice living and, trust me, I've had lots of practice.

Remember, the goal isn't about not feeling the things we feel—it's about not getting trapped in the thinking and beliefs that those feelings might represent. We did end up replacing those cars, twice. Because all the hoopla was never about them anyway.

> "Remember, the goal isn't about not feeling the things we feel—it's about not getting trapped in the thinking and beliefs that those feelings might represent."

For our 30th wedding anniversary we took a road trip to North Carolina. This was a state neither of us had ever been to and we were excited for an adventure. One of my favorite chefs and TV personalities at the time had a couple of restaurants in a little town on the eastern side of the state, so after we toured the Biltmore home in

Asheville, we headed to Kinston. First up was the fancier restaurant of the two where we dropped some serious dollars, but it was for our anniversary so that's how we justified that. As we sat at dinner in the midst of the five or six courses, Kelly asked me what I would do if my chef-crush Vivian walked in. My quick reply was, "She won't, she's on a book tour." Listen, I know things.

We finished our fabulous meal and drove the 30 minutes back to our hotel. When I say this was a little town in eastern NC, population 20,000, I'm saying there was nothing remotely close by other than the second restaurant, which we went to the next day for lunch. As we were enjoying our warm banana pudding in a mason jar, we were talking about what it was about this particular woman that drew me to her. It wasn't just her, it was people I saw who were not in their twenties, but had lived a little life, and they were leaving one thing to start another—taking risks, stepping out in faith. At the time, it was the season of life I was in as well. I was 50 and, after having spent all of my 40s in full-time ministry, I was without a job and wondering what was next.

As we sat there discussing my attraction (not in a weird way, just admiring) and groaning against our very full bellies, I heard a laugh from across the restaurant that I knew instantly was hers. She was clearly back from her book signing and was picking up some food. Kelly encouraged me to go introduce myself. Absolutely no way on God's green earth was I going to be that person. But my dear hubs reminded me that maybe it wasn't about me, what if it would bless her? So, I worked up the courage to walk over, introduce myself and she was as kind as I hoped she would be. She came over to the table, introduced herself to Kelly and coerced a local businessman who was innocently eating a burger at the table next to ours, to take our picture. She walked away, I excused myself to go to the bathroom and promptly burst into tears. As in, sobbing. I wasn't feeling any of the things that normally made me cry, so when I got back to the table, Kelly helped me walk through the "mad, sad, glad" process. I identified I wasn't really sad, I was afraid I would never be able to figure out what would be next for me.

Later, when I had time to reflect on the interaction with Vivian and my reaction—what I sensed God saying to me was that He had more for me in my future than I could ever imagine. Wouldn't you know it, when I asked Him what I should do, "You can trust me," is what I sensed. Unlike the trust He was inviting me to with the cars and Kelly, this trust was more about God's creativity. It felt like an invitation to remember that my imagination was endless, all I needed was a spark to reignite it. So, I've been working on that.

In the years since that encounter, my world has been a bit upside down and back again. Losing jobs and parents and friends and a home will do that to you—but until I get a different word, I will keep leaning on what I know to be true, because He told me so. God has more for me than I could ever imagine and my job is to keep living faithfully today, so when tomorrow comes I'm ready.

Shame, fear and anger aren't going anywhere for me. They will be in my emotional repertoire forever, because as a friend told me once, "We don't fail in new ways." I'm also confident that joy isn't going anywhere either—it's kind of like the other three have a "plus one." Knowing that these four will be with me for a long time, I have gone on a journey to learn how to trust them. God gave them to me for a reason and I happen to think His motives might be connected to His ongoing invitation to become more like His Son, my brother, Jesus.

TO CONSIDER

What lie have I believed about trusting my emotions as a guide to healthier living?

What truth could replace this lie?

What will knowing this truth change about the way I'm living?

Because change isn't a solo undertaking, who, among my trusted friends can I tell about this discovery?

Exhibit C: Drama is More Than a Club in School

Jerry Elton Stover was my high school English teacher. He directed all of our plays and musicals at school. My sister was in theater, as was my brother and they both had, and still have, beautiful singing voices. When I showed up, I think Mr. Stover thought he knew what he was getting. However, while we Robbins kids could act, not all of us could sing. I will never forget what he said to me when I auditioned for *Finian's Rainbow*, "It's a good thing you're so over the top dramatic, because you sure aren't a singer." We could always trust Mr. Stover to be honest, painfully so at times.

This wasn't the first time, nor would it be the last, when I would think that I needed to somehow cover up the fact that I was lacking something, somewhere. Some kids went silent when faced with their deficits, but I got louder and then I got rewarded for it. I got a part in that musical and every show I auditioned for from that point forward, even though the singing parts were pretty rare. While I had a lot of fun with the dramatic parts, my drama wasn't just for the stage. I loved to tell a good story, embellish it if necessary, and often made myself either the hero or the victim. What I didn't have words for at the time, but knew was true, was that I was lacking something essential, way down deep inside me where no one could see, and this missing "something" was a certain kind of confidence connected to belonging. So, I got bigger and louder and "more." What nobody, even me, knew was I expanded myself in all the ways I could, because I expected most people would sooner or later see the fractured thing inside of me, that I didn't know how to fix, and they would leave me.

It would be decades after Mr. Stover sliced me with his words until I would be introduced to a tool that would help me dive into the motivating factors behind my insecurities and lack of confidence and climb back up to a more truthful and compassionate view of myself. I still feel those old feelings of "lack" sometimes. Not as much anymore, but it sometimes happens right before I drift off to sleep or in those moments before I'm fully awake and before I know it, I'm thinking that my innermost being beyond repair and because that's true, I don't fit in anywhere.

One of the best men, and bosses, I've ever met is Wayne Feay. He is a peacemaker, the kind of person I feel safest with in the world. Before we ever met, he served in the military, then was a missionary in Sierra Leone, and then came back to the States to be a pastor. When our paths crossed he was the executive pastor at the church where I would be on staff for nearly a dozen years. I was 40 and he was the age I am now. He wasn't quite old enough to be my dad, but he had enough life in the rearview mirror to be the guide I needed on my journey at the time.

"This is the core wisdom of the Enneagram—not to just identify what you do, but rather to understand why you do it and how you might grow in doing some things less and other things more."

Wayne had a way about him that some found kind of "standoffish," but I never experienced it. For me, he was calm to my chaos, practicality to my whimsy, and a steady reminder when and if, I ever forgot who I was. He made me take days off, he advocated for me to lead, and was my champion with the denomination when it came time to get ordained. He also introduced Kelly and I to the Enneagram.

Now, before any snap judgments are made, I just want to say this about the Enneagram—I hated it at first. I didn't get it, and I thought it was a complicated web of numbers and lines and labels and wings and finger pointing. So, after a year or so of trying to understand it and how it could help us, we said, "Thank you very much, but not for us." Wayne was fine with that, in fact I think what he said to us was something about it just not being the right time in our lives for it. I remember thinking, "Yea, I'm not sure it's ever going to be the right time."

Jump forward almost a decade and I find myself wandering around in that emotional and relational desert I've talked about before. I was experiencing a kind of poverty—not only in my relational world, but in understanding myself and my purpose. It was in this season of tumultuous transition that my friend, Allyson gently asked me if now might be the right time to revisit Enneagram. She was a therapist and used it pretty heavily in her practice. For whatever reason, this time the Enneagram was the right tool at the right time.

Kelly and I signed up for a two day workshop in Nashville, TN and sat under the teaching of a woman who I had no idea at the time, would become not only one of the most influential voices on my journey, but a trusted friend. For two days, Suzanne taught us in a simple and straightforward manner and as she did so, my heart and my head began to lean into what she was saying. I started to feel like I might just begin to recognize myself again and if I could do that, I might be able to offer myself some grace and compassion that had been lacking for quite awhile.

Ennea means Nine.

Gram means graph.

Enneagram means a 9 pointed graph.

There was no witchcraft or mind control (Google it, people say these things) that I've been exposed to, but it is old. My Catholic friends tell me there's been conversation about the Enneagram as a part of their tradition for over 40 or 50 years.

Evangelicals have jumped on the bandwagon recently, but those who take Enneagram work seriously understand that it's not something to be memorized or conquered and then treated like a trick performed at parties. Instead, in all the training I've received, I've consistently been invited to think of the Enneagram as a process one enters into, in order to better understand one's true self. I've grown to understand it to be a source of wisdom, understanding, and compassion—first for myself, and then for others. Unlike other tools used to discern personalities, Enneagram is not based on preference. Rather, my core type (which is one of the identifying numbers 1-9 I most strongly identify with) is determined by my motivation. For instance, one of my daughters and I both struggle with pleasing people, so it might look like we're the same number, but the reasons behind WHY I seek other people's approval are connected to my need to belong, Katie's are tethered to her need to be needed in order to be loved. Same behavior, two completely different reasons. This is the core wisdom of the Enneagram—not to just identify what you do, but rather to understand why you do it and how you might grow in doing some things less and other things more. As Wayne used to often say, "Enneagram is just there to help you catch yourself, being yourself."

However, lest you think this is a "sales pitch" for Enneagram and any minute I'm going to hit you with, "Click on the link in my bio," I want to let you know why I'm talking about Enneagram. I'm sharing this here, because with the language that the Enneagram provides me, I understand myself and my relationship to my emotional intelligence more than I ever have in my life.

Enneagram uses the numbers one through nine to identify what is called a core "type." The numbers don't hold any value per say, as in, One is better than Four, and Nine isn't higher than Six. They're just numbers. My core type is an Enneagram Four. I knew this 15 years ago when Wayne Feay introduced my husband and I to the tool and I know it today.

Here's the best description I've got for an Enneagram 4, written by Beatrice Chestnut, PhD in her book called *The Complete Enneagram*:

> *Core type four represents the archetype of the person who experiences an inner sense of lack and a craving for that which is missing, and yet can't allow for the attainment of what might provide satisfaction. This archetype's drive is to focus on what is lacking as a step to regaining wholeness and connection, but through an over-focus on the experience of a flawed self they become convinced of an inner deficiency that prevents fulfillment.*
>
> *The natural strengths of type fours include their large capacity for emotional sensitivity and depth, their ability to sense what is going on between people on the emotional level, their natural*

feel for aesthetics and creativity, and their idealistic and roman-
tic sensibility. Fours value the expression of authentic emotion
and can support others with great care, respect, and sensitivity
when they are experiencing painful emotions. Fours are highly
empathic and can see the beauty and power in painful feelings
that other types habitually avoid.[5]

Until I had this language in my life, I never understood why I could sit with someone who was suffering and not have to fix it, just be with them. I was confused by my ability (and sometimes physical need) to find beauty in things others were just walking by without a second glance. I didn't comprehend the dynamic in me that caused me to long for deep connection and so I would draw close to people, only to pull myself away if I have any inkling that harm might come my way. I am now able to reflect back, without shame, to the little girl I was who would try to bring comfort to herself (by sucking my thumb and rubbing together anything nylon) because I felt so deeply different and "other" in my family. For years, even after I became a Christian, I couldn't shake the sense that something was irreparably broken inside me.

I've heard people say that Enneagram 4s are the most compli-cated core type on the Enneagram. I believe it. I have had contempt for the things I've learned about myself and at the very same time, I have discovered things about myself that have allowed me to breathe again. It's like the excitement that comes with a brand new box of crayons, that will never dull, and the colors I know are being laid down in my heart and head and body are spectacular.

For the last several years, I've been working out where the things I'm learning about myself and my personality fits with my faith as a Christian. I'm not all the way there yet, but I'm pretty convinced that if you look at all nine of the types at the absolute best version of themselves, you will catch a glimpse of the Triune God—Father, Son, and Holy Spirit.

- Ones are looking for the GOOD in the world. Who does that better than Jesus?
- Twos are working out ways to HELP each and every person

they come in contact with. I can't think of a better helper than the Holy Spirit. Threes are driven and drawn to getting it DONE. Wasn't it Jesus who said, "It is finished?"

- Fours have an unending longing to CREATE. I do believe all of creativity rests in the One who flung the stars into the heavenlies.
- Fives are hard wired to KNOW, and there is only one omniscient Father.
- Sixes are absolutely at their best when they are SOLVING problems, and as far as I know, there isn't a question whose answer doesn't reside in the heart and mind of God.
- Sevens are most content when they have the freedom to PLAY, and that kind of joy can only find its origin in the Holy Spirit.
- Eights are in their wheelhouse when they are someone's ADVOCATE and that is best reflected in the role the Holy Spirit plays in our lives and in the Kingdom.
- Nines are constantly seeking PEACE, for themselves and others and there is only one Prince of Peace.

The Enneagram isn't for everybody. I'm aware of that and it's just fine. I'm also aware that we all need something—a tool, a method, a process—that allows us to experience greater self-discovery and to grow in our social, emotional, and relational intelligence. With a deeper awareness of ourselves, we not only begin to trust our thinking, feeling, and doing, we can continue the journey of becoming the amazing human beings God saw inside us when we were fearfully and wonderfully made. If we go on that journey, we get to invite others to do the same and that sounds like a pretty great life.

I have often thought about what my life would have been like if I had possessed the language and knowledge that goes along with a tool like the Enneagram, all those years ago when Mr. Stover told me not to quit my "day job." I'm guessing, I would've been able to calibrate more quickly than I did then, I think I carried that hurt for the entire production of that play, and I'm confident I would've been able to speak up for myself—reminding Jerry Elton that I never pretended to be a singer anyway, for me it was always about the DRAMA!

TO CONSIDER

What lie have I believed about my personality?

What truth could replace this lie?

What will knowing this truth change about the way I'm living?

Because change isn't a solo undertaking, who, among my trusted friends can I tell about this discovery?

PART 6: TRUE SELF

LIE

*If people really knew you, the real you,
they wouldn't choose you.*

TRUTH

*There is no need to fake it until you make it. Your true self is
enough, and the journey that is required to rediscover who
that is is an adventure worth going on.*

Thomas Merton wrote, "Everyone of us is shadowed by an illusory person: a false self... we are not very good at recognizing illusions, least of all the ones we cherish about ourselves."[1] From the time I was a young child, I have been in the business of disguising my true self. This cover-up has required heartache, joy, loss, and, finally, being "found" for me to begin to uncover who I was always meant to be. I understand my "true self" to be that version of me that I was always meant to be by the God who made me. Some people call it your essence, some label it your authentic self, or your original self. This idea of the true self, the authentic you, can be found in psychology, sociology, and theology and no matter what you call it, it implies a journey. Because as soon as we are born, the "me" God intended for me to be—perfect, without flaw or any liabilities—ceases to exist. Consequently, we spend much of our life doing the work of returning to that original version of ourselves which the Bible calls, "Fearfully and wonderfully made."

To have your mother's eyes or father's nose is one thing, but to be made in the image of the Creator of the world, well, that's pretty spectacular. And yet, I haven't met a person who doesn't have a story of wearing some kind of mask or burying a part of who they really are as a way of protecting themselves or, even more heartbreaking, trying to hide a really important part of who they are. I did that. For years, I pushed down and shoved back my authentic Suze. I would catch glimpses of her here and there, but it wasn't until I came to the end of myself, laid down the fake stuff and picked up the genuine, that I discovered something that's always been true: my true self is enough and the adventure of discovering who that is, is worth it.

The evidence offered here suggests that we don't have to be anyone but who we were always created to be. To put a mask on only covers over the beautiful me, the beautiful us, we were always designed to be.

"Any hope that you can know yourself without accepting the things about you that you wish were not true is an illusion. Reality must be embraced before it can be changed. Our knowing of ourselves will remain superficial until we are willing to accept ourselves as God accepts us—fully and unconditionally, just as we are."

DAVID G. BENNER[2]

Exhibit A: Who Are You Anyway?

I get called a lot of names: Suze, Mom, Susie, Momma, Sass, Pastor, Wifey, and Susan Elizabeth, if I'm in trouble. In my nearly six decades of living, I've also had a variety of roles and responsibilities; daughter, sister, friend, granddaughter, girlfriend, wife, mother, professor, enemy, business owner, pastor, vice president, unemployed, outsider, insider, Cancer-girl, and more. Over the years I've learned what is required to carry out the duties and responsibilities of all of these things.

I've jumped through a lot of hoops and checked off the requirements from a variety of lists. I tried to learn what it meant to be successful as both a mom and a college professor. The requirements proved to be similar and very different at the very same time. To be an accomplished business owner, I was taught I would have to be tenacious, firm, and driven. The list for wife, and one who would remain committed to one man for the whole of my life, did not include the same rules of engagement as any of the other roles I was taking on. The list could go on and on, suffice it to say in all that learning about what rules to follow in order to be successful at "this" or "that," I ended up forgetting who Suze actually was. I spent so much time trying to DO the things you DO to be a daughter, a pastor, a Cancer survivor (or at least what I thought was required) etc., that I forgot how to BE me.

If I ever truly knew.

Having survived the parenting of three teenagers, I can say with confidence that it's normal for kids to start the investigation into the "who" of themselves in their tween years. Not to try and sound too analysty, but I think those early teen years, for all of us, are the beginning of asking, "Who am I?" and, "What's my purpose? " It may not be that clear and definitely not concise, but it looks a little bit like starting to pull away from the parents and siblings, if they exist, and flexing the muscle of "self." I was no different.

I attended a small midwestern high school. Back then, because there were under 500 of us in four grades, if you wanted to, you could do a little bit of everything, and I wanted to. During my four years, I played volleyball in the fall, basketball in the winter, ran track and played tennis in the spring. I had parts in the fall play and the spring musical. I was a little bit above average student who had some leadership gifting, so I was in the National Honor Society and a class officer. Choir, the yearbook, and intramurals were also part of the landscape for me, and that was just school.

I was also a part of our local Youth For Christ club, I attended Church every Sunday with my family, I was part of a traveling drama troupe for a time, and was active in my own youth group and the youth groups of my friends. I started working as a dishwasher in a local diner when I was 13 and have had either a part-time or full-time job for all of the 44 years since.

I lived a life crammed to the rim with doing. When I look back at those days I'm mindful that this level of activity was pretty normal. I wasn't the only one this busy—all my friends were as well. Back then, there weren't many club leagues or travel teams or drama camps to attend. So, I signed up, joined, auditioned, and created all the activities and responsibilities I could find. Partly because that's what you did, and partly because I was somehow convinced, and no one was telling me different, this would be where I might figure out who the real me was. I was also just one year, and then two years, and then unimaginably three years post Cancer, and I was determined to live the life I had been given full tilt.

As a side note, I'm also convinced that it was Cancer, and all that it cost us during the year of diagnosis and treatment, that kept my parents from saying "no" to me very often during those high school years.

Don't get me wrong, it was fun. I had a blast doing all of this with my friends and classmates. However, as I look back, I'm also deeply aware something was being formed way down deep inside of me. A certain kind of belief about myself, that to be valued and liked and worth "it" (whatever "it" was in the moment) I needed to not just be busy with things, it was imperative that I be outstanding in all that I did or tried. This belief that I needed to be clever and funny and smart and heard and busy shaped both my childhood and my teen years in ways that are easier for me to describe than it is for me to fully understand. It's not as if anyone was standing over me saying, "You better be the best." Instead it was like when the choir is singing and a beautiful high soprano solo line comes floating in the air—you're aware it's there, you're just not sure where it's coming from.

One of the things all the busy achieving sparked in me was people pleasing, and it started at a very young age. Before I was participating in sports or auditioning for plays, I was driven by the desire to please others. I wanted to please my mother, my piano teacher, my Brownie leader, and my pre-kindergarten teacher. Oh my word, my pre-k teacher—I loved her deeply. She was the most beautiful woman my little four year old self had very seen, with the most perfect afro, that I longed to touch, and the largest bosom, that to be drawn into and allowed to rest against at the beginning of our morning together was just about the best part of every one of my days. I would have done anything to make her proud.

And that's the heart of it for me, I started young and kept approaching the world with a "what would you like me to do or say so you will like me?" attitude, and in doing so I lost sight of my real self. I've shared plenty in these pages about my journey of discovering the "real Suze Fair." When I look back at all that activity and the early longing to please, whether the motivation for it was to be closer to my Mom, to try and figure out my place, or to get a big, squishy hug from my teacher, all I know is that my desire to be liked and chosen has been there for a very long time.

Lately, I've been sorting out some things about my true self. The real me. The part of me that is my essence, my identity—the threads that God created and wove together—which means He is the only one who can make modifications. I think, and I'm pretty sure I'm not alone in this, my true self started to get covered up in the very early years of my life. From the first time I cried as an infant and didn't get the response my little baby mind was longing for, I've been trying to gather information about the world and make sense of it. Consequently, in the midst of all those crazy, busy formative high school years, whatever remnant of my true self remained after childhood, got buried underneath all that frantic doing. The other part of my theory is that it might take me a long, long time to uncover all that got buried, and I'm OK with that.

You've already read about my season of working in a church. It was a pretty big (2500 people more or less) community and I got to serve as the Director of Expression and Experience. I led a team of creative folks I loved deeply, I sat on the leadership team, and preached every now and then. Our kids were 14, 12, and 9, bringing along with them all that those ages require. My dear husband was also in the midst of a fragile season of recovery from a diagnosis of clinical depression. I felt weary and pulled too tight. Something felt fractured inside of me and I was striving for a certain kind of elusive peace that seemed just out of reach. I was in therapy with a trusted counselor who has proven to be an important part of our family's journey for many years. What got me back in her office initially was my need to please, but what kept me there was the realization that all the busyness in my world was no longer helpful to my mental, physical, emotional, and spiritual health. Rather than adding more, I needed to start subtracting. Instead of covering up, with people-pleasing, achievement, and the affirmation of others, I would need to do the hard work of revealing more of who I was actually made to be, by learning how to stop and say no.

What I learned in this season is that God reveals in order to heal, and what was being revealed would prove to be a significant step toward rediscovering my true self. I started to wake up to the fact that it wasn't going to be the busyness or achievements of my younger self, or the ability to make others happy, that would give me the "success" I so desperately wanted in all the places that mattered to me. Rather, to become the wife, mother, friend, or pastor I was hoping to become, I would need to access the qualities of an intentional, loving heart, mind, and soul; love, humility, curiosity, a willingness to be wrong, the ability to lay down my right to be "right," faith, and a forgiving heart. It was time to stop trying to become someone or something different inside each of those spaces and just be me, Suze Fair.

Being me is deeply-rooted to my discovery of my identity. My true identity was profoundly tied to my ability to see myself as God saw me. I started that work of discovery with my 42-year-old bottom in a therapist's chair and yet it would be another 10 years before I untangled the lie that my worth and value was contingent on my human DOING rather than my intrinsic value as a human BEING.

Even after all these years, I'm not sure how one comes to the place of truly believing she has worth and value without a faith and belief in someone bigger than oneself. For me, that someone is the God of the Trinity. God, Jesus, and the Holy Spirit. These three have worked in me, on me, and with me powerfully on my journey of rediscovery. Like the gentle and honest Parent, Sibling, Spiritual Guide they are, I have felt nothing but invitation as I've stepped deeper and deeper into this "knowing."

> *"Even after all these years, I'm not sure how one comes to the place of truly believing she has worth and value without a faith and belief in someone bigger than oneself. For me, that someone is the God of the Trinity."*

Trust me, I've brought buckets full of shame to this relationship, and yet, still just an ushering to more—of me, them, life, and love.

In the spring of 2015, I was in the early days of my 50s. I had been in ministry for a decade, two of our three kiddos had left the "nest," and all that weariness and longing had finally caught up to me. I asked the church leadership for a sabbatical and my request was approved. Ninety days away to rest and renew my spirit, my mind, and my body. What a gift.

I went to the beach for a month. The first week, the family was with me, and then, they all left and I found myself by myself. The very thing every mother wishes for when her children are young. In those days, a vacation is not a vacation at all, it's just all the responsibilities of real life in a place where all the "go-tos" for consoling hurt feelings, fixing up skinned knees, and refereeing another sibling war about fairness, are nowhere to be found. I can't count the number of times I told my husband in those days, "My dream vacation would be me, all by myself, at the beach without anyone else."

Then it happened in the form of this sabbatical, and I was a disaster. I cried for the first three days after they all left. What had I been thinking? Who thought me being all by myself for a month was a good idea (that was me by the way, I was the one who thought it was a good idea)? What was I going to do with all this time by myself?

After those first couple of days, things calmed down and I found myself in a rhythm that was actually restorative. I arrived at the beach thinking this time away was going to be about sorting out some complicated things that had begun to surface at work. Instead, there were other things that needed to be worked out. This time would be about my understanding of two things: God's love for me and how far I was from who He had actually made me to be. That sabbatical, like the wise counsel I received in my early 40s, would be another step in the journey of rediscovering my true self.

On Day 11 of being on my own, I wrote in my journal, "Today, I woke up with so many feelings and they kind of scared me. I was feeling envy, worry, sadness, fear—out of a dead sleep, I felt all of that. Oh God, what is happening to me?" As I've shared before, I am a person with A LOT of feelings on a regular day, so take me away from all that is known to me and my routine, and all of those emotions were clamoring for some attention. As I laid there and explored what it was I was actually feeling, I realized the envy was connected to other folks I knew who had gone on a sabbatical and come home with clarity about things that had been a mystery when they left. Convinced there was a "right" way to participate in a sabbatical, my worry was connected to my fear that I hadn't figured out the formula for success and it was all going to be a bust. My sadness was connected to words that had been spoken to me by one of our children, at home while I was gone—we were missing each other. All of these feelings were like a big dark cloud over my head that I had no control over. Would they break open and the storm would fall or would they move on and the sun would return? What I didn't know then, but I would later discover was this exploration of my emotions and the power I do or don't give them over my life would be a HUGE part of why the Lord invited me to take the risk of a sabbatical in the first place.

On Day 12, something shifted inside me and I remember this as being a break-thru day. At the end of that day, this is what I wrote in my journal:

"Yesterday, all day, I felt God calling me to something. Inviting me to three things: to Be Still, to Be Small, and to Be Brave.

To Be Still and know without any doubts that He is God. Fully sovereign. He sees it all, He has control of it all and no amount of my activity or "crazy making" doing can add to that. When I'm tempted to DO (to prove, to woo, to convince, to coerce, to cajole, to control, to...whatever) I hear God calling me to trust. So I can BE (faithful, humble, obedient, prayerful, loving).

To Be Small. This is a challenge for me. To shrink, not back but really to take the place that was meant for me—so that God can increase. God is so BIG. Universe Big. Savior of the World Big. My heart, mind, & soul Big. My puffing myself up with opinion, gossip, or manipulation can't diminish Him, it only diminishes me. And diminished, I can't take the place He has planned for me. Every time I'm tempted to insert my opinion, myself, my misguided emotions, I hear God challenging me with His BIGNESS. "I've got this and you Suze Fair. You must decrease, so I can increase in your life."

To Be Brave. To be courageous, in all the ways that really matter, is my deepest longing. To trust God, so fully and completely that I will follow Him wherever and whenever. To pray. To speak. To be silent. To go. To wait. To serve. To be "for." To stand against. To be still. To be small. To trust God's BIGNESS in the whole of my life. I'm convinced this will cause me all kinds of different and difficult.

Oh Lord, what is the pathway to this life? How do I get there?"

Be still, be small, be brave.

All these years later, these three "Be" phrases are what keep me connected to the journey that is taking me back to my true self. Today, I live in the awareness that I am not any of the names someone might call me, and I can't even seem to find the version of myself I was so enamored with inside the roles I've taken on or served in.

What I was being invited to on Day 12 of my Sabbatical has proven to be the greatest, most difficult adventure of my life so far (even more than Cancer). To Be Still when everything inside me wants to fill my life up with so much busyness that the discomfort I feel when I'm not "producing" or adding the world's version of value somewhere gets skipped right over. To Be Small when everything in me is fighting the urge to jump up and down, wave my arms and yell in my outside voice, "Hey, it's me—don't forget about your girl over here." To Be Brave when I'm so very scared of running out... of influence and joy and trust and money and health and belief.

My identity isn't something anybody on the outside of me gets to decide (not even me). Like the treasure it is, it was buried inside me, when all that would be Suze was getting knit together inside my dear mother's body. I'm committed to spending the rest of my days on the journey of returning to that precious gift, the authentic version of me that no longer needs to hide behind "busy."

TO CONSIDER

What lie have I believed about my true self (identity) when I look at it through the lens of my activities and responsibilities?

What truth could replace this lie?

What will knowing this truth change about the way I'm living?

Because change isn't a solo undertaking, who, among my trusted friends can I tell about this discovery?

EXHIBIT B: YES. GIRLS CAN DO THAT

The first time I remember being excluded or treated differently because I was a girl was in the sixth grade. It didn't happen at home, although my parents had some pretty traditional patriarchal "stuff" happening; it happened at school. Looking back, I wouldn't have been able to tell you it was a gender thing, but it was. My sixth grade teacher was Mr. Larimer. I adored him. He was kind and yet firm and seemed unaffected by all the drama that gets attached to kids in that age group—girls starting to like boys and hating their bodies, boys starting to not trust their voices and trying to figure out what to do with those just-starting-to-emerge "feelings" for girls. Mr. Larimer was in charge of all the AV equipment for our elementary school. When I say AV, I'm talking about Audio Visual machinery. Things like overhead and slide projectors, tape recorders with giant ear-muff headphones , and film projectors. Here's the way it worked: if a third grade teacher wanted to have a slideshow in her classroom, she would put a request in with Mr. Larimer and one of his students had to get it prepped and delivered. It was a big deal to be chosen for deliveries. If you were delivering one of the overhead or slide projectors, you had to make sure the bulb worked and there was a cord; if it was good to go, you wheeled it to the appropriate classroom. However, if a film projector had been ordered, you had to load the film, make sure the lens was in focus, the bulb was working, and of course the power cord was there. Delivery of the film projector was viewed as crucial to the ongoing success of the Leo Elementary Audio Visual department. There was an unspoken understanding that only the most responsible students would get chosen for that job. Nine times out of ten, a boy was chosen for the delivery. I'm not saying Mr. Larimer was sexist; I have no idea what his thinking was, this was 1976 and while Gloria Steinam was having a very public impact in the women's rights movement elsewhere, it sure wasn't happening in the halls of Leo Elementary School. Whatever his reasons were, every time Mr. Larimer called on Greg, Thom, Marty, or Jeff to take that film projector to a classroom, I felt slighted somehow, overlooked because I was a girl. These feelings would bury themselves inside me and I would feel them again and again as I navigated the world.

I've worked professionally for over 35 years. I've been a part of start-ups and well established corporations. I've served in higher education and the local church. The only context where I've never experienced gender biasing, whether it was subtle or overt, has been when I worked for myself and even then, I had to deal with it from clients. However, lest you think this only happens in the workplace, I've also experienced it in the context of family and friends.

I'm aware that in my work and personal life, I've overlooked and excused plenty of bad behavior by men, because I didn't want to cause a ruckus or I was just flat out afraid for my job or my place in a relationship. I've laughed at jokes made at the expense of women, I've accepted less money than my male counterparts were receiving, I've looked the other way when I heard a man speak or act inappropriately to a female on the team or in the family. All of that happened in my 20s and 30s, but then I turned 40 and something happened inside me and I just wasn't having it anymore.

I was getting ready to leave the university setting and step into full-time church ministry. As part of the interviewing process, the church had me participate in a couple of personality assessments, conducted by a highly regarded consultant. After I completed the assessments, this consultant met with the senior pastor, who would have the final say as to whether I was hired or not. The consultant advised the pastor not to hire me based on what he had seen on the assessment. He told the pastor, "She's aggressive and opinionated. She'll want to be in charge and we don't want that to happen and I'm not sure you [the pastor] can handle that strong of a woman."

Ummmm....

I'm sorry, what?

Two thoughts: I have no idea why that senior pastor sat me down, for what I thought was going to be my final interview, and instead shared the consultant's recommendations with me. This sharing wasn't actually helpful to me in any way, causing me to start my tenure in a defensive posture, with something to prove. It was only with the Lord's protection that I kept my cool for the remainder of the interview. We talked through it and the pastor indicated to me that he still wanted to hire me. I think I said something about not agreeing with the recommendation, and then I accepted the job.

But, underneath the surface in a place where neither that consultant or pastor would ever see, I was raging. I knew, without a shadow of a doubt I had hit some kind of wall inside me. I was thinking of all the times I had smiled at a male colleague's inappropriate language or behavior or had laughed, even if it was nervously, at an off-hand derogatory comment or joke at the expense of someone in the minority. Those comments by the consultant and the conversation that followed felt a little bit like when you're in a dead sleep and someone starts shaking your shoulder to wake you up; it can be jarring. That was me, I don't think I realized how "asleep" I actually was to the misogynistic treatment of myself and other women I cared about. It took me a while to respond to the shaking and find my voice. Figuring out how to actually act when all those bad behaviors surfaced again—because they did—felt like an uphill unlearning. The truth is, you don't spend 40 years thinking and acting one way, flip a switch, and it's all new.

Sadly, my resolve would be tested again and again in the church where I began my full-time ministry work. One of the first times I ever preached on a Sunday morning, a gentleman came up to me afterward and told me he couldn't hear a word I was saying because he was distracted by a piece of jewelry I was wearing. "Never have to worry about that with [insert male pastor's name here]," were his exact words. Part of the leadership structure at this church was a group of lay men, called Elders, who were elected to provide oversight and support to both the staff and the church body. Every staff member was assigned an Elder who was supposed to meet with him/her on a monthly basis. My first assigned Elder was a kind man who talked to me like his daughter, not as a leader who carried responsibilities for both team development (seven staff and over 100 volunteers) and a significant chunk of the annual budget. My second assigned Elder was uncomfortable meeting with a woman by himself, so our meetings were sporadic and when they did happen, we talked about our families and vacations (or some other benign topic) in order to keep our conversations "appropriate." I had male colleagues who would make decisions without the input of the female team leader who was ultimately responsible for the implementation of that decision. When I asked those male colleagues why they acted in a way that felt diminishing toward these women, their response was often, "That's not how I meant it," or, "I was just trying to help."

I wish I could tell you that my response in those situations was always bathed in curiosity and kindness. It was not. Sometimes I lost my cool, sometimes I cried, and sometimes I just withdrew. Underneath these emotions, though, what I wanted to communicate was some version of, "I know you're not a bad guy, it's just the tone, the "iffy" joke, dismissive attitude, or the bypassing of the qualified woman you serve alongside." I loved these men, they were my brothers in Christ and they could do better.

In the 17 years since I made that decision to not look the other way anymore, I have worked in a variety of settings. I have worked inside organizations led by men who professed to be Christians and wanted to lead Christ honoring organizations. I have experienced all of what I'm talking about in every place I've worked, and in the later years, I encountered these things as a leader at the executive level.

Even with all the moments I've experienced in all the places where they've happened, one of the hardest things for me to understand is the church and its ongoing issue with women leading. The marketplace, while it still honks me off, I can comprehend. Societal culture made decisions about a woman's place, either at home or at work, that females have been fighting against for decades. But the church? I don't get it. Why does this institution, that I love deeply, seem to be a better reflection of the world's view of women and their "place," even though society still has miles to go when it comes to gender equality, than Jesus'?

Trust me, I've heard all the arguments and read all the papers and books (well, not "all," but a lot) and I still land in the place I've always resided: Jesus did not hold one gender in higher regard than the other.

So, why do we?

The reason I offer this here is simple—I have children who all have incredible gifting, given to them by the God who made them, and the church needs them to not give up on her. Whether our daughter's feel called to full-time church ministry or there are partners or friends or granddaughters someday who do, my hope is that my children will do the work that is required to sort out their own view of how Jesus treated both men and women. I'm actually cheating a little here; I do believe the offspring have already done a lot of this work, so maybe it's actually for others I care deeply about. To be clear, this is not an attempt to persuade or "win over" people's thinking about gender equality in or out of the church. This is just my story, and my story is of a young woman who thought she knew what she thought about equality between the genders, women leading in the church, and what God had to say about both of those topics. Instead, this young woman (me) had to wake up to the fact that she didn't really know what she thought or what God said about either the equality or the leadership matter. So, I sent myself to "school" when it came to learning and discovery on this matter. I read books, I had conversations, I built friendships with *"If you don't know what you think about politics and religion, racial reconciliation, divorce and remarriage after, human trafficking, human rights, or the role of women in leadership—the only place I know to go is to Jesus himself."* other female leaders, I studied scripture, I went to conferences, and I prayed —a lot.

Today, when I encounter someone who is trying to sort out where they stand on an issue pertaining to their faith or what they should do about a decision in his/her life, I often say, "If you don't know what to do, or how to respond, do some research and find out what Jesus would have done or how he might have responded. It's all in the Book, you won't have to look very far." Sadly, lots of people I know are unwilling to do that "work," especially when it comes to gender issues around equality and church leadership. Instead, they stay with what they've always known or with how the majority culture is "handling" the topic.

If you don't know how to respond to poverty, find out what Jesus did.

If you are struggling to know what to do when someone you care about receives a bad diagnosis, go find out what Jesus did.

If you don't know what you think about politics and religion, racial reconciliation, divorce and remarriage after, human trafficking, human rights, or the role of women in leadership—the only place I know to go is to Jesus himself.

Here's what I know about Jesus and his view of gender equality, and pretty much any other "hot topic" that got thrown his way: he was often counter-cultural and mostly counter-intuitive.

When it came to women, Jesus pushed against societal norms and spoke freely and publicly to women as equals. Think about Mary and Martha, the woman at the well, and the woman who had been suffering physically for years and reached out to touch the hem of his robes. Whenever Jesus spoke to anyone, except for those rascally money changers in the temple, he was a gentle teacher. He was a rabbi and the Son of God, so it would have been in his nature to be thoughtful and caring in the way he spoke. With women, his voice was described as gentle and intentional and he often called them "daughter," even though some of them might have been close to him in age.

The Apostle Paul wrote a lot of letters, to a lot of different churches. This was his way of continuing to shepherd them, even when he was half a continent away. One of the themes he touches on, repeatedly, is equality—equality among slave and free, Jews and Greeks, men and women (among other things). Where would he have learned this, if not one or two or all of the 12 disciples who walked with Jesus?

When I think about the ways I have been made to feel "less" as a woman in the church, it's never been from Jesus. I've never had a moment during worship, reading my Bible, or in the quietness of solitude with God where I have heard a message that sounded like, "Suze, we think you're great, amazing in fact, except for that part of you being a girl...that, we're really not thrilled with." How could this be true, when the Bible tells me I was made in God's image and there is no distinction for that status based on my gender. The writer of Genesis says it this way:

> *So God created mankind in his own image,*
> *in the image of God he created them;*
> *male and female he created them. (Genesis 1:27)*

Nope, the times I have been made to feel less have been by being at the other end of comments and actions made by men and women in the church. It's pretty sad really, to be at the receiving end of the kind of exorbitant grace that gets handed out so freely to God's children and then what we shovel out to each other is often sexist nonsense.

I've long held the view that if the church could get in alignment with how Jesus thought about and treated women, lots of other "issues" might just sort themselves out. In an article entitled, "How Jesus Viewed and Valued Women," James Borland, ThD says it this way:

> *Jesus demonstrated only the highest regard for women, in*
> *both his life and teaching. He recognized the intrinsic equality*
> *of men and women, and continually showed the worth and*
> *dignity of women as persons. Jesus valued their fellowship,*
> *prayers, service, financial support, testimony and witness. He*
> *honored women, taught women, and ministered to women in*
> *thoughtful ways.* [3]

I couldn't agree more.

I'm profoundly grateful for the handful of men I've met—Wayne, Ken, Brian, Chris, Stephen, and of course Kelly Fair—who have done their own work around this issue and settled for themselves where they stand. To be clear, I've never told a man in the church that he and I needed to agree on this in order for us to get along or be friends—instead, all I have asked and will keep asking is that men would "do the work" for themselves and decide what they personally think.

Here's what I know: to learn how to navigate in the church, let alone work in one, I have had to decide first what I think Jesus' approach to gender equality might be. Then, I had to decide that my worth and value just couldn't be decided by or connected to my intelligence, my status, my experience, my gender, or whether or not the world sees and agrees that I am the beloved Daughter of the Most High King. I know who God says I am and it has nothing to do with what an Elder Board or a senior pastor or a church consultant might say.

Gosh, I'm glad that's true.

Someday, I hope the Church works out its "stuff" with gender equality, but I'm not holding my breath. Instead, I'm going to remain clear on what I know about myself as a woman in leadership and what I know to do as a disciple. I'm going to keep asking God what He's saying to me, what I should do about it, and then I'm going to do it.

TO CONSIDER

What lie have I believed about what the culture (or my family or my church or work) says about my gender and what I can or can't do because of it?

What truth could replace this lie?

What will knowing this truth change about the way I'm living?

Because change isn't a solo undertaking, who, among my trusted friends can I tell about this discovery?

EXHIBIT C: "FAKE IT TIL YOU MAKE IT" ARE NOT WORDS TO LIVE BY

I used to love to pretend. As a child, I had an imaginary friend. My mother used to tell me that I could keep myself occupied for hours by playing nonstop games of "school" and "house" and all the variations (school bus, school room, supper time, cleaning, etc.) that came with those games. My imagination was, and still is, incredibly developed. That's not a braggy statement, it just is. Back then, I could imagine a classroom full of students, today I can imagine a garden in full bloom or the details of a family vacation.

Ask my husband, and he'll tell you that I often kick off a conversation with, "Wouldn't it be great if...." I'm not saying those musings always become reality (rarely), but it's still fun to let my imagination go sometimes. I've always thought a high sense of imagining is just having the ability to let your thoughts meander around for a while and then having the discipline to let them wander until they discover something new or creative or beautiful. As a friend always used to tell me, "Dreams are free."

Currently, and I've had this happen before, I am emerging from a season where it felt like my imagination had gone to sleep. As hard as I tried, I struggled to dream or even start a "what if" thought and follow it all the way to the end. This usually happens to me, in my professional life, if I spend too long sitting at a desk in an office somewhere from 8:00-5:00. In my personal life it can happen when I isolate myself from others or stop listening to great music, reading well-thought out stories, or watching a great movie. It's like all the color drains out of the painting of my life and everything goes to gray tones. Often, in these times when my imagination goes dormant I am tempted to pretend that all is well, life in the monotone is not as bad as I think it is, or if I don't say, out loud, anything about my creativity being dormant then it won't be true. Not exactly the healthiest version of me.

Right now, I've been able to create some room for myself and healthier life rhythms again, and in that space I feel like I'm returning to myself. I can feel my imagination coming back online.

After church a few weeks ago, I was having a conversation with an incredibly talented young man. An entrepreneur, married to his high school sweetheart, and dad to two little sweeties. In our conversation, he said to me, "Suze, have you ever heard of imposter syndrome? I think that's me." I told him that yes of course I had heard about it and we talked about what might be triggering this for him. What I didn't tell my young friend was that I have experienced this on and off for the entirety of my days. I didn't always have a name for it, and actually I didn't need one, because what I have felt has been so deeply a part of my story for so many years. I'm not sure I can remember a time before age 12 or so when I didn't feel like I was not who everyone thought I was.

Imposter syndrome is a thing. Even though some of us (me) hadn't heard of it until a few years ago, this reality for many, was given a name in the late '70s. It was first described and identified by psychologists, Imes and Clance, as the Imposter Phenomenon, and was typically attributed to high achieving women.[4] Today, it is now acknowledged as being widely experienced—across gender, socioeconomic, and racial categories. It's described as an internal experience where you believe you are not as competent as others perceive you to be, you don't belong where you are, and have only gotten there through pure luck and circumstance. It's a booger, and something I think we'll be talking about for a long, long time.

I'm guessing this syndrome will be with us for the foreseeable future because there are very few of us who know how to believe in or act like our true selves. How many times have I said, "If you only knew the real me, you wouldn't choose me?" A lot. I'm pretty sure the distancing between the truest version of ourselves and the ability to believe innately in ourselves, begins when we are very young. For instance, if someone, a parent, a friend's dad, a Sunday school teacher, or a coach, responds to us in a way that causes pain or harm, we step away from being the little girl or boy who trusts everyone and believes everyone is for her good. Even if that step is subtle or small, we are still moving away from our purest selves, not toward her.

Some of us have had to deal with deep physical, sexual or emotional trauma, and my heart is broken over that. Others of us have been traumatized in other ways; a divorce, a diagnosis, or a move across the country away from our best friend. Whatever it was, and there's never just one thing, these events act just like a thunderstorm that rolls in on a hot summer night. Our survival depends on us running for cover and so, whether the hurt is big or small we run. What gets covered up in that running is the real me. All the while, the truest version of myself is still in there, trying to make herself known. Like a teeter totter, I can find myself going back and forth between, "I bet I can do that," and, "There's no way on God's green earth I can do that." This is when I feel most vulnerable to bumping into that imposter syndrome—"If you only knew the battle that was waging inside of me right now, you would never trust, believe in, or welcome me." Consequently, over the years, I created a false self. A version of me that would keep anyone else from seeing the war of doubt, insecurity, fear, or even apathy.

If I was going to list for you the "storms" that have rolled into my life and caused me to create a false self, I wouldn't know where to start. My parents were married for 63 years and loved each other deeply. I, along with my two siblings, felt loved and well cared for. We went on vacations, and my parents bought a lake cottage so our summers were pretty great. I had friends, we went to church, I adored my fraternal grandparents, and it seemed like I might be kind of smart. So for me, the journey away from true self wasn't one big thing, it was incremental moments, small pokes and injuries. Things like, having a parent that was hard to please and, as you've already discovered, I was a pleaser. Living in a household where there were a lot of pretty tight boundaries, I often stepped right up to them and sometimes crossed over (somehow I always got caught and punished). In my family, intelligence was highly valued and everyone was smart, including me. But I always wondered if I was "smart enough." My mom was motherless when she had me and that, as I now know, rips a hole in a woman's heart that takes a lot of work to repair. I had teachers who were demanding. Looking back, some of them crossed the line of appropriateness. One of my friend's dads got up and left their family when we were very young, and for a very long time I was deathly afraid my dad would do the same. These moments, little by little, seemed to be the evidence I needed for it not to be safe to be my true self. I'm not confident it was always a conscious decision, but I can tell you, when I look back and see myself pretending to know something when I didn't so I wouldn't get caught not knowing or to go miles out of my way to gain someone's approval, I see the pattern of true self cover up with great clarity.

So, was it any one thing? Nope. But that's the point, it doesn't take a cinematic plot line to cause us to drift and turn to run away from our true selves. I learned in increments, not all at once, to "fake it" until I made it. It wasn't until I was older that the dilemma emerged: How would I know if I had made it, and when would it be OK to stop faking it?

Every time I started something new—a class, a semester, a job, or a project—I would get a stomach ache. Who would I sit with? What if I can't figure out the information? Who am I going to eat lunch with? What do I do if I fail? When will someone find out I have no idea what I'm talking about? These are the questions that pestered me for decades. It wasn't until I began to live a life of less covering and more transparency that I could leave "what is" and launch out into "what might be".

In my 20s and 30s, I spent an awful lot of energy worrying about getting "caught" not knowing something. It didn't matter whether I was presenting to a client or teaching in a college classroom, I was sure I was one unanswerable question away from being found out. It didn't matter what letters were after my name or how much experience was in my rearview mirror, this insecurity hung with me until I was in my 40s. I became weary and worn out. Through the loving kindness of my husband and a few close friends I acknowledged that, in order to not be a person who impersonates someone who has it all figured out, I had to just stop.

To get over it, I had to go through it.

So, I started saying things like, "I don't know", and, "Honestly I've never heard of that." When I got an assignment that I truly had no idea how I was going to finish, instead of trying to figure it out on my own, because I was scared of rejection, I began to have conversations with my friends, family, and my boss about capacity and limits. I had spent years nodding my head when I was clueless and making up answers that sounded good, just to protect myself. So I stopped the empty head nods as well.

It was like I implemented a cease and desist on my false self, on the version of me that had been masquerading as the actual me. It was rough but so very worth it because, for the first time in any time that I could remember, I felt free. Free to be myself, nothing more and nothing less. Lots of people had no idea I was covering up; I had been doing it long enough to be really good at it. But I knew it, and I also knew that the shame I had been experiencing as I worried about whether I was presenting myself in such a way to be liked was exhausting, and I was ready to lay it down.

I haven't met very many people, even the one I look at in the mirror, who have stopped pretending they are something or someone they're not. It requires a lot of effort and time, and even after all the work, I think we're still tempted sometimes. That's OK.

I had an assistant when I worked at the church, and her name was Autumn. She had also been one of my students when I was a professor, so I knew her pretty well and was excited to work with her. She was kind and generous and funny, gosh was she funny (she's not dead, so she still is), and she was a great audience for the jokesters that were on our team. Everyone felt better somehow when Autumn was around. If she said she was going to do something, she did it. If she took on a project, I knew it would be creative and well thought out. One year I was doing her annual review. There honestly wasn't anything I could offer in the way of critique, so I had to stretch for improvement goals. I think I said something like, "Autumn, you're one of the most self-aware people I know. Everyone trusts you and is glad when you're in the room. You are a stellar human, just don't stop being you." Autumn responded by telling me she didn't really understand what I was saying, she wasn't doing anything special, she was just doing the work that needed done. "Don't try and figure it out," I said, "just keep being Autumn."

Most of the time, due to all the covering up and faking it, we tend to forget who we really are. Autumn hadn't done that, and we were all better because of it.

When I was deciding whether I should leave a job I cared deeply about, I was struggling to know what to do. I had probably held on too long, and I could feel myself starting to get frayed around the edges. My relational world was getting wobbly, and I wasn't quite sure about my place anymore. Into this process, of what would eventually lead to my leaving, I invited some trusted advisors to help me process. We spent an evening together talking through where I was emotionally, mentally, and spiritually and what my next steps might be with the job. When they started to offer me some counsel, I got my pen out to take notes. One of them told me they felt prompted to point me to the story of David and Goliath. I resonated with this—what a story of faith and belief in the face of the unknown. Another, encouraged me to examine if I had forgiven my boss for the hurt I had received. This was such a good word and, as soon as it was said, I knew I still had work to do around forgiveness. Then, one of the friends told me they felt, because they were convinced I couldn't do hard things, this potential leaving would probably require lots of faith. And just as quickly as I knew I should spend time reading about the giant and the shepherd boy. I should also make a list of hurts to be sure I had fully walked through the forgiveness process.

> "Sometimes being true to the real me, means I can't believe everything I hear, even if it's from people I love."

I knew what this person was saying was not true. I did (and do) know how to do hard things.

I was tempted to put my head down and agree. To pretend again. To act as if I agreed when I didn't. I was already feeling so deeply exposed so, in order to protect myself, I could act like this statement hadn't cut me to the core as it had. But I didn't. I took a few days to gather my thoughts, write them down, and then ask the group to come back together. When we gathered back in our living room, I shared what I had learned from them but also what I disagreed with. I was grateful for the input, but they weren't right about all of it.

Sometimes being true to the real me, means I can't believe everything I hear, even if it's from people I love. That moment of knowing what was and wasn't true about what my friends were sharing was a powerful one. I could see myself as someone who had changed. I had moved from being a person who needed to hide her true thoughts and ideas and just "go along to get along," to being someone who could ask for input, weigh it, and then respond authentically. There were moments of trusting myself before, but this one was a big one and would define a season of change that was coming—job, faith community, friendship loss, moving—in a way I could never have imagined.

It felt as if I was putting "fake it til you make it" behind me, and for that I'm grateful.

TO CONSIDER

What lie have I believed about the ways I have "faked it" in order to make it?

What truth could replace this lie?

What will knowing this truth change about the way I'm living?

Because change isn't a solo undertaking, who, among my trusted friends can I tell about this discovery?

Exhibit D: Journey Back to Suze

In the early spring of 1993, Kelly and I walked into a split level, smoke-filled home to meet our son for the very first time. Benjamin was exactly 45 days old and had been in foster care for that entire time. He was well taken care of despite the second-hand smoke ear infection already brewing in his body, and we couldn't wait to take him home. He was ours. This baby we had been begging God for the last many years was here and home. When we loaded him in the car on that very windy Michigan morning I climbed in the backseat, looked at Kelly in the rearview mirror and didn't know whether to burst into tears or gut busting laughter. What in the world were we doing? You can beg God for something, He makes it a reality, and still have no idea what you're doing. That was us that morning (and honestly for many mornings that followed). I have a crystal clear memory of Ben starting to cry on the toll road between Michigan and Indiana. With no tools in my "Mommy can make it better" toolbox yet, I made Kelly pull the car over and switch me spots.

We made it back home and began what still continues today: learning Ben. One morning I was on the floor next to him as he was lying on a blanket and, as I got lost in that kid's eyes, I thought, "I wonder who you're gonna be?" My next thought was, "I wonder if I'll have what you need to help you get there?" We had been through all the adoption classes and home studies, paid all the money (thank you, Mom and Dad for the co-sign), unwrapped all the "stuff" that babies need, yet, there we were—just the two of us with one of us asking the question I think every parent probably asks.

I've been through this three times now, staring into those brand new eyes trying to see if I can catch a glimpse of the future them. It never worked; what I saw instead was the miracle of who they were. In the early moments of their fresh and new selves—so recently arrived from being in the presence of the One who had fearfully and wonderfully made them—their pureness was fully on display. In those early years of parenting, I had just begun my own journey of returning to a state of fearful and wonderful. I was often in the death grip of a "I'm going to completely screw these children up" fear.

Ben is almost 30 now, and his sisters are 28 and 24. My role as "mom" has changed significantly, and mostly I'm glad about that. What hasn't changed is my longing to see them find their own unique way back to the essence of who they were when God placed them in whoever's womb they grew in. Because that's where I believe our True Selves are created, and it's not until we enter the world that it starts messing with you (when I say "it," I mostly mean parents who don't know what they're doing).

This idea of rediscovering our "true selves" has been around a long time. Read anything by David Benner, Richard Rohr, Thomas Merton, the desert Mothers and Fathers, Brennan Manning, Frederick Buechner, and the list goes on and on. But in my life growing up no one was talking about this idea. You were who you were. Mostly that theory proves to be fine, unless you're a kid (or teen or adult) who doesn't really like or know who they are. What about them? As I've shared in other places here, I grew up with a deep sense that something was flawed in me, and if people really knew me they would never choose me. This thinking was broken, as is true with most things that get broken and not tended to right away, you forget it's not what it was or should be. Like a screen door that lost its spring and slams every time someone goes out the door, my heart and my head forgot that to feel fatally flawed was nowhere close to "fearful and wonderful;" it had just become my normal.

I spent a lot of years trying to cover up what was happening on the inside—all that confusion, feeling like I didn't belong, carrying an oddness around with me—by over-trying to be normal. If you knew me back then, you might even tell me I did a pretty good job. But what I didn't know, and again no one in my world was talking about it, was that I was creating a false self—some version of me that I thought would be more acceptable, more welcome, and easier on the seating chart. It didn't really work though, for me that is. I think it worked just fine for the world around me. I got married, was employed, had friends, became a Mom, got asked to lead in the church and in businesses, was a teacher, and accomplished a thing or two. This worked for me until it didn't, and that's when I knew change needed to happen. I needed to do the work around shedding my false self and embracing a truer version of me, the version God dreamed about when He put me in my mother's womb. I referenced it often in these pages—but much of my life in my 30s and 40s was about waking up to the fact that I needed to go on a journey back to Suze Fair, who she really was and who God had always meant for her to be. I was old enough to know that the work required to initiate the kind of change I was looking for wouldn't come from a book or a workshop or a TED talk (trust me, I tried). Instead, this transformation would come from self-discovery and being in community. The first thing I did was tell Kelly and a few others. Then, I went back to therapy, left a job that was not the best environment for me to be my true self, created new boundaries, took the drugs when I got clinically depressed, gave myself time before I jumped back into full-time work, and spent time with scripture and my journal every day. Change like this, the inside-out kind, can be slow at times, and in a hurry-up culture like ours it's tempting to give up or say, "Good enough." Father Richard Rohr talks about the journey away from our false selves like this:

> Our culture is almost entirely prepared to not just help you create your false self, but to get very identified with it and attached to it. So, without some form of God experience, which teaches you who you are apart from that—we would say in the religious world, who you are "in" God, in the mind and heart of God—there's almost no way to get out of it.[5]

For me to persevere on this adventure back to my true self, I had to first decide that there was a really good person waiting for me there. A version of me who was like those fresh and new babies of mine, trusting all that was before her was for her good.

Early in this process, a friend asked me to write a letter to my six-year-old self, a version of me that had yet to begin to believe that if she wasn't extraordinary or followed the rules exactly, there would be no place for her. Here's an excerpt from that letter...

Dear, sweet brown-eyed girl,

I just wanted to tell you that I think you're amazing—just the way you are.

You're funny and smart and beautiful—but that's not why you're amazing.

You're amazing because you're you. You don't have to DO anything for that to be true.

I love the way you color outside the lines and pound on the piano while you're "writing" your songs.

I think your imagination is awesome. Keep inviting your pretend friend to dinner and tea parties.

You don't need to pretend though when people ask you how you are, if you're scared—tell them you're scared, if you're happy, say that.

You have a natural spark that makes people want to be with you. Don't try and figure it out, just be you.

I know there's lots of rules and stuff in your house, it's OK— they're there to keep you safe, not because you're in trouble.

You are so very loved. Mom loves you a lot even if it doesn't always feel like it. Dad thinks you're pretty special too. Your sister loves you and wants to protect you and your brother loves you lots, even when he's off with his friends playing and you're not invited.

I cried buckets when I wrote that letter. It felt like such a tender, loving thing to offer myself and words I, most likely, had been waiting nearly fifty years to hear. It was all true, and still is: I was and am loved. Did my family love me perfectly? No. Did God? Yes, a thousand times yes. It was such a healing exercise, like a balm on an old, old wound. Like the beginning of the repair on a long-forgotten broken screen door.

About three years into my journey back to Suze adventure, I went to work at a private equity firm. It was a job, at a time I certainly needed one, and I was grateful. I had begun to separate myself from the thinking that "the job makes the woman", and I was able to enter into the corporate culture pretty freely. I met some amazing people and was offered the opportunity to interact with some wonderful self-development opportunities. On the surface, it seemed to be about as far away from ministry as I could get, but it wasn't really. There are broken people everywhere, parched from the demands of living and looking for a cold cup of water. During one of the team development times, I had my journal out and was just jotting down what I was hearing when, smack in the middle of a presentation (which I couldn't tell you the content of now), I heard, "...because you have nothing to prove, nothing to lose, nothing to hide...." I couldn't tell you what was said before or after that, because as I wrote down and stared at those words in my journal I remember thinking, "If this was the only thing that comes from this job, it's all good."

There have been moments that have led to real transformation on this journey back to my true self. All along the way, I have been required to allow my false self to fall away from me. Like a snake going through its annual molting, I had to decide to not pretend, to not lie, to say "no" when everything in me wanted to scream "yes" to get someone's approval, and to just keep moving forward with accountability, vulnerability, and honesty. This journey has been about discovering that my true self, my essence, is the version of me that has nothing to hide because I have been hidden in Christ. There is nothing left to prove because Christ got up and walked out of a grave to prove that death will not have the last word. What could I lose when everything I am and have is God's anyway?

Remember when I said this was a journey? Well it is. I didn't get fully embedded and tethered to the not-completely-authentic-version of myself overnight. It took me decades of not paying attention, ignoring the promptings to turn back to Truth when they came, wanting other people's approval more than God's, and all the other paths that lead me away from that beautifully made brown-eyed girl. So it would take me a bit of time to return to my true self, and I would need people along the way to help me. My husband has proven to be the greatest voice of reason and my greatest encouragement to keep journeying toward my true self. In the process of writing this book, I have forgotten more times than twenty why I was even doing it. Recently, as we were working in different places, I called him and said, "I'm struggling with 'what's the point' thinking about this book." I was discouraged, frustrated, and scared." Why was I spending all this energy, time, and money for something that wasn't going to be published by anyone but us, read by a handful of people who cared and the people in my family I arm wrestle into doing so (dramatic, I know)? I confessed to Kelly that I am tempted in every way to just quit. His response? "Well, if you were doing this because you have an agenda like attention or fame I would tell you to quit. But that's the old you, not who you really are." The minute he said it, I knew he was right. The easy thing to do would be to stop, the right thing to do is finish. Not because of what I'll gain, but as an act of obedience.

> "*The easy thing to do would be to stop, the right thing to do is finish. Not because of what I'll gain, but as an act of obedience.*"

When I think about how far I drifted from my true, fearfully and wonderfully made self, there's no one to blame. I'm not that kind of gal. If there's any one person or any one thing to point to, it's just my life. My life with all its beautifully broken glory has provided an invitation to pretending and living authentically. I just happened to choose to pretend longer than I should have.

Just for the record, this journey back to my "fearful and wonderful" status is never truly over until I go home to Heaven, where I actually belong. I'm believing that by the time I get there, I will have trusted God and the journey enough to lay it all down and hear Him say, "I would recognize you anywhere. Welcome home daughter."

You know, I was uncomfortable every time my Dad told me to, "Walk in like I owned the place," and that fake it til you make it mindset was a part of my approach to living for decades. The truth I now know is that there is no need to pretend to be someone I'm not, because the someone I am is pretty spectacular. I also know when I am weary and worn out I am most tempted to hide behind a false version of me. I hope I never let that happen again. But who knows, I might. Life's hard, and sometimes we return to patterns and ruts in the road from our past navigation of difficult stuff. Mostly we do that returning because we can't see a new way forward. For me, these are the moments that require the most honest and authentic version of myself. If I keep inviting her to the journey, who knows, I just might make it.

TO CONSIDER

What lie have I believed about exploring how I might have created a false self?

What truth could replace this lie?

What will knowing this truth change about the way I'm living?

Because change isn't a solo undertaking, who, among my trusted friends can I tell about this discovery?

PART 7: THE PLAN

LIE

If you have a good plan, you'll get the life you want.

TRUTH

God's plans are better than ours. He can be trusted.
With everything, always.

I have always lived in a culture, which includes my personal and professional life, that seems to live and die by a plan. There are people who become strategists as a profession and help other people build out their one-year, five-year, and ten-year plans. I like a good plan as much as the next girl, but I have learned over the years that a great plan for your life does not equal getting the life you are dreaming of. A great plan may mean you do get the degree, the partner, the family, the promotions and the 401K. It could also mean you don't.

When I look at where my life is now and then look over my shoulder to where my life has been, it seems to be true that the best plans for my life have come from the heart and mind of God. I could never have written out the story of how my life would go, let alone captured it in a set of life goals. Plans change, often. Sometimes I have finished last when I was sure I would be first. The husband and I have found ourselves down to very little money in our bank account. I have made decisions that seemed so "right" in the moment, but proved to be a source of deep failure and pain.

The evidence presented in this section opposes the world's lie that the plans we make are the best and the ones we need to stick to—no matter what. The Bible's not kidding about much, well anything really, and when it says that God's plans are better than ours and that His ways are not our ways—those aren't throw away statements, they are words to live by.

"*We suffer to get well. We surrender to win. We die to live. We give it away to keep it.*"

RICHARD ROHR[1]

EXHIBIT A: GOD CAN BE TRUSTED (IN ALL THINGS)

The Christmas I turned 28, we told our families something I thought we never would: we were pregnant. As I shared in an earlier chapter, we were dumbfounded that after years of doctors, drugs, and too many tears to count, we had made a human. On the advice of many, we waited until we were past the "risky" part of the pregnancy (the first trimester) to tell. We wrapped our 10-week ultrasound in Christmas paper with a big red bow and had our parents open it.

Best Christmas ever.

Two weeks later, our doctor put one hand on my knee and another on Kelly's shoulder and let us know that our sweet baby boy's heart was no longer beating. We could either wait for my body to naturally expel the fetus or I could schedule a Dilation and curettage (D&C).

Worst start to a New Year ever.

In the overflow of that heartbreak, Kelly and I earnestly began to ask God for something that felt bigger than asking Him for a child; we asked God for a family legacy. Would He do it by expanding our family with children (in any of the ways children can come to a family) or would we have children at all? However God was going to do it, we longed for something that would outlast us. We hoped for children, of course, but we were living in the grief that comes from the best laid plan not working out the way you think it's going to. Part of our healing would be to turn our hearts to the biggest kind of trust we knew. Would we be able to trust God for a family when we were so deeply disappointed and sad?

I was raised by planners. My Dad approached pretty much everything in his life with a "measure twice, cut once" philosophy and he filled dozens of yellow legal pads with notes and lists and calculations. Mom had what seemed to be a blueprint for every home improvement project, family gathering, as well as how she was going to arrange her furniture. I don't have any memories of us jumping in the car for a spontaneous trip anywhere. Growing up, the last word you would use to describe either of my parents would have been impulsive.

This approach served my folks well and, if I had to guess, I would think they might have told you it was because of their careful planning that they had the life they had—a good one with lots of love, generosity, achievement, and plenty of stuff. This planning life is what I knew and it was what I had observed, but as I got older, it didn't seem to be working out for me exactly like it did for Mom and Dad. Or maybe, I just wasn't close enough to see the gaps and cracks in the execution of their plans. As often happens when you look at someone's life from the outside in, all you can see is what's lying on the surface—the fancy new house or the child successfully graduating from an Ivy League school. If I find myself concluding that a person's life is going according to plan because of the pictures that get posted on social media, I'm not looking deep enough.

I've had a lot of plans over the years that I was counting on leading me to the life I thought I wanted (dare I say deserved?), and rarely have those been the way things went. I had plans to be a lawyer, because I really liked the character of Joyce Davenport on the TV show from the 80's called Hill Street Blues. This was not a good enough reason to spend that much time and money getting a law degree. I had plans to be single until I was in my 30s, live in a big city, and travel the world. Married at barely 21, with a degree that was so ordinary it was difficult to find a job, we lived in a midwestern town of about 50,000, and counted our trips back to Indiana as our vacation. I had objectives for my health, our bank account, and the makeup of our family. None of those have gone according to my plans.

It took me a long time to get untangled from the lie that when my life turned away from the route I was hoping it would go, it was because I didn't have a good enough plan—or that I didn't have a plan at all. Instead, I had to begin to explore the idea that maybe, just maybe, God had a better plan for me and that all the details of that plan were His alone to know. In addition, even when there was an absence of what I felt was necessary information, God could be trusted.

When we miscarried that baby in 1992, I was at the earliest stages of learning to lean less into my will and way and more into the ways of God. One would think, after three decades of attempting to walk in the way of Trust I would have it figured out. One would be wrong. To this day, I still tend to fight, dig in, or otherwise question when my plan starts to unravel. Over and over I've had to decide and keep deciding that God can be trusted with the people and things I care about.

When our kids were in elementary and preschool, we found ourselves living off one very small income. By "living" I mean we were barely getting by. We were in a season of healing as a family, and it didn't make sense for both of us to be working. We were trusting God to make a way where there seemed to be no way, and it was stretching us. About six months into this season, my dad

"I'm learning how to embrace the truth that the life I am meant to live is going to have its ups and downs. I will win and lose. My life will have its seasons of confusion and clarity, and plenty of joy and sorrow."

was asking how we were doing. I updated him, and he asked about our dwindling money situation. "So, what's your plan for that second job?" Dad asked. My response was that we were praying about it, trusting God, and waiting for Him to move. "Yea, I get that, but what's your plan?" Dad replied. At that moment, it was so tempting to start scrambling, making lists and calls, and shaking all the bushes we knew to shake—when we had clearly felt prompted to wait. If we had made that mad dash toward employment, we would have missed all the moments God had ready for us as He worked out His painfully generous plan in that season of our lives.

I don't want to come across as cheezy, but this was a season of low funds and high faith, and we now think of it as a time of great blessing. If we had run back to work, we would have had no need for my brother and his wife to loan us their second car, always full of gas, so Kelly could drive two hours each way for counseling. Each time Kelly came driving home in that car I was reminded of God's goodness when you need it most but you don't know how to ask for it.

With both of us at work, we would have not been there to pay attention to the way God was giving us room to heal. He seemed to be protecting us in the smallest of ways, like making a trip to Target, the grocery story, or the car pick-up line at school and not running into anyone connected to the source of so much of our pain when.

We would have been at work when Kelly's dad called and asked to meet for breakfast. This was kind of an unheard of thing in their relationship, so we didn't know what to expect. After Kelly left to meet his Dad, I was getting ready and God said in my spirit, "He's going to give Kelly a check for $5,000", and that's exactly what happened. What Kelly's parents didn't know was the night before we had prayed over our last $100. We would have missed the unexpected blessing of them giving us that gift, if we had scrambled to make our plans work instead of waiting on God's.

In the book of Isaiah, the Bible says that the way God thinks is not the way we think, and His way of acting is not our way of acting (Isaiah 55:8-9)—that's good news to me. In the New Testament, Matthew says God is an excellent parent who has good gifts for his children (Matthew 7:11). In fact, God is the only parent I'm aware of who will never harm His children. He can't cause harm, it's not in His character. So, because God's thinking is above ours we can be confident that while His way of working things out might not be the way we would want it to be, His way is always right and good.

I've been on a journey to replace the lie that tells me I have to have a flawless plan for my life to be the one I'm longing for. Instead, I'm learning how to embrace the truth that the life I am meant to live is going to have its ups and downs. I will win and lose. My life will have its seasons of confusion and clarity, and plenty of joy and sorrow. With that in mind, the plan for my life is not as complicated as I think it is. That plan is to keep listening to the One who, thinking we were a good idea, breathed us into life and doing what He says. Not an easy plan, but most definitely doable.

Don't get me wrong, I've wrestled plenty with this idea of God's plan being better than mine (and nearly impossible to figure out). In fact, as I type this, I'm trying to figure out what in the world God is up to in my life and the lives of lots of people I love. But my inability to follow along or to comprehend the plan doesn't mean God's got it wrong or is going to leave any of us high and dry. It just means He's the Creator of the Universe, the One who hung the stars in the sky and carved the Grand Canyon out of the earth, and starts and stops a beating heart. I'm choosing to believe that because He figured all of that out, He's got the sorting out of my life covered too.

TO CONSIDER

What lie have I believed about God's trustworthiness?

What truth could replace this lie?

What will knowing this truth change about the way I'm living?

Because change isn't a solo undertaking, who, among my trusted friends can I tell about this discovery?

Exhibit B: Plans Change

When we head out on a road trip it is often my job to pull up the map on my phone and get the directions to our destination. My map app always gives me multiple routes for my chosen destination. Without fail, I always pick the fastest route. You may not do that, but I do. Without even looking at the details all I see is "fastest" and I chose that one. Mostly, it ends up being a good choice, I mean, who wants to get somewhere in an hour and 47 minutes when you could arrive in an hour and 34 minutes? Those 13 minutes are impossible to get back.

I say mostly it's a good choice because sometimes I click "fastest," against the advice of the driver, who is almost always the husband, and it ends up being a convoluted set of directions with every possible turn, detour, and two lane road possible. Looking at the screen, it seems like the smart thing to do, the most efficient way to get to the destination, it looks like the right plan. Then you get out on the road, all the unexpecteds happen, and the trip ends up taking twice as long as it should have. Then, the one holding the map gets to say those three excruciatingly difficult words, "I was wrong," more than she would care to.

Life's like that too I think. More than once I have thought I had a great plan, for the day, for an event, for life, and sometimes that plan seemed to be working out exactly the way I hoped it would. Then, in an instant, everything changes. I mean, everything. With one small shift, you can be four years into a five year plan and it all (or at least it seems that way) blows up.

My dad was a planner and taught me to do the same. Granted, I wasn't nearly as tied to the plan as Dad was, but I have, over my nearly six decades, made a lot of plans. Vacations, moves, jobs, relationships, projects, illnesses, my children and their futures. All of that has received the benefit of my, "If we do this, and then we do that, we will get there", kind of thinking. However, in my many years of walking around on this planet and making those plans, I've also learned that all it takes is one broken down car to wipe out your savings account, one failing grade to plummet your GPA, one diagnosis to derail nine months of vacation planning, or one lie to destroy trust between friends.

When my husband turned 40, he had a breakdown. In all the ways a human can break. Emotionally, physically, and spiritually, he broke. At the time, he was in year seven of serving as an associate pastor alongside what he would have called one of his closest friends. It was a smaller church, but growing, which meant that the two guys, a worship pastor, and a part-time children's pastor were in charge of it all. Because of the growth, the church sold its building so a bigger one could be built and became "portable," which meant that every week two trailers full of gear had to be unloaded, set up in the gym of a local middle school, and then after church all that gear had to be torn down and loaded back into those trailers. Kelly Fair was in charge of all of those moving parts and that, on top of his regular responsibilities, began to take its toll on him. In the winter of his 40th year, he and I found ourselves in a strange and painful place in our own relationship. We were friends and co-parents and roommates, but not much more. Our level of intimacy was as low as we had ever experienced in 15 years of marriage, and my heart was breaking a little bit more each day as time marched forward and not much changed.

One night in early January of that year, I asked him if we could talk about our relationship. After the kids were in bed and we sat down to talk, I brought the only question that was in my heart, "Is this as good as it's going to get between us?" Without missing a beat, he looked me right in the eye and said, "Yep." One word that even now, when I go back to that living room and see those two having that talk, I can see and feel the lights turning off in my eyes. Little did we know that in just a couple weeks, it would all break apart—a bad job review for Kelly would lead to a lot of confusion and questions with that pastor/friend, which would lead to the pastor and his wife and four boys to distance themselves from us, which would result in a spiral down into depression for Kelly, which caused him to start to flail in the job, which then triggered a leave of absence, which would end in the loss of the friendship, the job, and our faith community.

This was not the plan. At all.

We then entered into a season of unraveling that would cause both Kelly and I to examine every nook and cranny of our lives. The first priority was Kelly's mental health, then we tackled our marriage, and then we looked deeply into the ways we were parenting our three kiddos who were ten, nine, and four at the time. Finally, our relationship with full-time ministry and how we had unhealthily connected it to our worth and value got examined. Kelly left full-time ministry for five years, and in that season, we found our way back to each other. As a result of this horrible time, and with the assistance of a lot of loving, wise counsel, we became the people we both knew we were meant to be but just couldn't seem to ever become. The reason for "not becoming" was 100% due to the barriers we kept putting up for ourselves, like unhealthy communication habits, passive aggressive behavior, laziness, and immaturity. We had never fallen out of love, but, during that season of examination and healing, our love became more than I could ever have asked or imagined. Everybody was better, and we were better because our plans had fallen apart.

Two years prior to his breakdown, Kelly clearly heard God invite him to a time of quiet and retreat. Kelly didn't do it. For reasons that are his to tell, he avoided a direct invitation from God and that, my friend, is never really a great idea.

My guess is, knowing God, there was some Good News He wanted to share with Kelly in that time away, but Kelly wasn't there to hear it. So, maybe the breaking that came later, was the best path for Kelly to finally be available to hear from God.

Isn't that how it is sometimes? The plans we think are good, are actually just safe, and the plan that is actually the best one for our lives, which may seem risky and dangerous, is waiting to be discovered in the midst of the brokenness. I don't think it always has to be that way. For me, it's proven more often than not that very little that is good and life-giving has come from trusting myself and my plans more than trusting in God's good and loving plan for my life.

My relationship with plans changing started when I was young, with that very first shocking diagnosis. All the things I thought I was going to do that freshman year, I had to lay down and make "getting to 16" the plan. Even at 15, I knew I needed to do whatever the doctors (and nurses) told me, not because I was a kid and I had to obey, but because that was the clear path to me getting better. I'm not sure my dad agreed. My dad was always a "the more you know the better the plan" kind of guy. My whole life, when he was making a decision, he made lists, did research, and considered all his options. All of this, in his way of thinking, would lead to the best possible outcome. In other words, the result he was hoping for. The truth that Dad had a hard time accepting was that no amount of listmaking or research or considering Plans A through F was going to make me well. The plan he had for my life was being radically changed, and he didn't get to be a part of making sure I would be around to write a new one. That had to suck.

> *"Isn't that how it is sometimes? The plans we think are good, are actually just safe, and the plan that is actually the best one for our lives, which may seem risky and dangerous, is waiting to be discovered in the midst of the brokenness."*

Dad and I talked about it years later, and he confessed that he was anxious a lot during that season. He was sure the doctors were not telling him everything he needed to know. For context, this was a teaching hospital, so every time a doctor came into my room, he brought with him nearly a dozen students. These "almost doctors" would gather around my bed and learn—about my disease, my treatment, and my prognosis. By the end of my stay, I felt like I should get some sort of diploma from all the information I heard flying back and forth across my poor, broken body laying in that bed. Poor Dad, he was always sure there was more to be known. So, after the lecture and the student Q&A around my bed, Dad would follow the doctor out into the hallway and say, "What are you not telling us?" Every time, the doctor would reply, "Not a thing. Not one thing." My dad had a choice to make, as we all do when plans change and things feel like they're spinning out of control: would he trust in the plan the doctors were laying out for me or try to figure out a better one himself? More importantly, would he trust that God had a great plan for my life and this season of sickness was part of that good, Godly plan?

Dad and I debated this, "If God is good, why do bad things happen?" question for years. After all the back and forth I'm not sure he ever really landed his plane on an answer he felt comfortable with. For most of us, and I'm not sure Dad was any different, when we start to entertain that question, the most natural next one is, "If bad things happen, shouldn't I actually trust my own plan more than God's?"

My dad was a man of faith, incredibly smart, full of confidence and doubts. He had a degenerative neurological disorder for which there was no cure, and he courageously held the disease at bay for nearly eight years. He had a great plan based on wisdom from his doctors, the latest drugs, and all the research he could get his hands on. I'm proud of Dad; he was tenacious about living life to the fullest for as long as possible. The potential problem is: he may have been tricked into thinking he was in control. It was a little like that GPS that gives us the fastest route, with no regard for all the potential roadblocks and detours that lie ahead.

I do believe Dad may have finally unraveled his question of God's goodness and good people suffering, and it happened as he was dying. All of us, his children, grandchildren, and his 90-year-old sister saw him embrace that there can be pain AND God can be incredibly kind and good. I'm convinced Dad struggled with this question until literally the day he died, and then...he didn't struggle anymore. What a gift to get to be with him when he embraced God's plan for his life as the very last words were being written in his story. Dad looked at me and told me he was going to be fine and he was going to "really enjoy himself."

Every time I forget that God's plans are better than mine, and trust me I forget often, there's a scripture that I scramble to look up (for the life of me I can't ever remember where it is) in Proverbs. I like the Amplified version of it best, "Many plans are in a man's (or woman's) mind, but it is the Lord's purpose for him/her that will stand (be carried out)." (Proverbs 19:21, AMP)

I have a lot of hopes and dreams.

I'd like my children to get to experience the lives they're dreaming of.

I'd like to retire early.

I'd like to visit all 50 states and several European countries.

I'd like to see my husband thrive in the business he has started.

I'd like to make a difference for the Kingdom of God.

I'm hoping to finish this book.

I long to grow old.

And for all of these, and all the other longings that have yet to surface, there's really only one plan: Remain faithful to the One who made me and put all those longings inside me.

If any of those things are going to become reality in my life, it won't because I'm working the right plan out, all on my own. It will be because the Creator of the world thinks these are a good idea for me and my people.

Plans change, but the One who makes it ALL happen never will.

I'm grateful.

TO CONSIDER

What lie have I believed about following a plan (or creating one in the first place) so I can have the life I long for?

What truth could replace this lie?

What will knowing this truth change about the way I'm living?

Because change isn't a solo undertaking, who, among my trusted friends can I tell about this discovery?

EXHIBIT C: MONEY TROUBLES

I hate money. There. I've said it. All the sayings I resonate with about money describing it in derogatory ways—the love of it is the root of all evil, it's a necessary evil, a penny saved is a penny earned, cash is king, burn a hole in your pocket—can't even come close to how strongly I dislike money. It's so arbitrary, pieces of paper, chunks of metal and yet, without it, you can't really navigate the world.

Don't get me wrong, when I have it and I want to buy something, my thoughts about money are pretty ambivalent. It's when we want or need something and the dollars are in short supply that my frustration starts to build. If you're close to me, it wouldn't be difficult to pick up on my money grumbling.

I'm not proud of this and I am working on it. This relationship with money seems to be pretty ingrained in me—so it may take awhile.

While my dad was a school administrator he also had a side hustle as a very successful insurance salesman. Right out of college, Dad started teaching high school math and coaching men's basketball. He was barely 22 and some of his players were 18, many of those boys went on to become lifelong friends. Soon into his career as a teacher, he and his closest college friend, Jim, went through training and began selling life insurance. Dad had a ready-made customer base, as soon as those basketball players graduated, he sold them a $25,000 term policy. My Dad built that avocation into a very successful revenue stream. It helped put all three of us through college, it paid for a summer home for the family, provided Mom and Dad with some pretty amazing travel opportunities, and allowed for a retirement with no financial concerns. While Dad was happily working those two jobs, Mom was working at raising us, making our house a home, and being as shrewd about saving a dollar as just about anybody I've ever met. Mom and I talked about it when I was an adult and she told me she always felt her financial contribution was to be careful with the money. She did that by cutting coupons, looking for ways to stretch her grocery budget, only buying quality products, and NEVER paying full price for anything.

As a kid, I didn't think my parents were stingy or tight with their money, I just knew they were careful. My folks used to tell this story about being on a trip to Dallas and going into the Stetson hat store. Dad really wanted a Stetson (he was a big fan of Louis L'Amour novels) and with the help of the shopkeeper he found one that fit. The Stetson guy had Dad step onto a little platform that was surrounded by mirrors, and as Dad always said when he was telling the story, "I looked pretty great in that hat Mim, didn't I?" Mom would smile and say, "Jim, tell them how much the hat cost." Well, that hat was $50, and in the early 1970s that felt like $500 to my folks. As Dad and Mom looked at Dad's reflection in those mirrors, Mom said, "Jim, do you know how many things we could buy with $50?" Their practicality won out, and Dad walked out of that store without a hat. Then, always as the life-lesson to the story, one of them would say something like, "Do you know how many Stetson hats we've said no to over the years?" If we were at the lake house when the story was being told, those "nos" would be the reason for their second home or if we were on a family vacation in Florida, all the Stetson moments would be the reason for the vacation. I had a love/hate relationship with that story. I loved that it was such an example of their willingness to sacrifice things that they wanted so they could do, or build, or pay for things that would last longer than a cowboy hat. I hated that story because it always made me feel guilty for all the "Stetson Hats" I had bought over the years, which clearly meant I didn't know how to manage my money (or at least that's how it felt).

As a kid growing up in what I know now to be a pretty affluent home, I don't think I really thought about a plan for money. I was trained early and often on WHAT you do with your money: tithe first, save second, and live off what's left. However, I was never really taught HOW to do that. While I nodded my head and agreed to this strategy while I was growing up, in all honesty, that approach hasn't always been the easiest for me to follow. It has never been that I don't know how to work hard, I've been doing that since I was 14, or that I don't know how to give or save. Also since the teenage years, it's that I see stuff I want and I get it. So, I guess you could say it's a discipline thing.

Before Kelly and I got married, we went through some pre-marital counseling provided by the campus pastor at the university we attended. This "counseling" consisted of a meeting with him where we talked a little bit about our relationship and our marriage goals. Then he had us take a personality assessment called the Taylor-Johnson, and at our second meeting with him we went over the results. That meeting was what we like to call a DISASTER. Looking back on it, I'm 100% confident his heart was in the right place, but his approach left something to be desired. He started the meeting with, "There are some results here I'm a little concerned about", followed by, "When exactly is the wedding?" Then when we reminded him of the date, "Would you be able to postpone it?" I was a wreck. Kelly held my hand and made me breathe, and we didn't go back for a third meeting. I'm not saying there weren't some things we needed to sort through. Trust me, there were plenty. It was the jarring opening statements that were upsetting.

All of that to say, there was absolutely zero conversation before our wedding, with anyone who might be able to guide us with wisdom, about what our roles and responsibilities might look like in the marriage. As we learned very quickly, there are a lot of things that have to get done in the world of adults, whether you're single or married, and without a mentor to guide us through who would do what, we defaulted to what we had seen our parents and grandparents do. "Girls do all the inside things and boys handle all the outside responsibilities plus the finances. This didn't work out so well for us. I had been too busy playing sports, going to drama rehearsals, and being sick to learn how to cook and clean. Kelly knew how to mow the grass, but we were renting Tipp Kardatzke's tiny half apartment, so that wasn't a needed skill. When it came to the finances, what we discovered was that there was a lot of incongruity in our approaches to money. It's not that we were opposed to each other, just vastly different in our thinking.

I've learned that the philosophy and perspective we have about money, and its role in our lives, has almost everything to do with how we were raised. If my family's approach to money was frivolous, I might end up being the same or I might become a tightwad. If the family's philosophy was all about saving for a rainy day (that never seemed to come), I might replicate that or maybe become the person who's always grabbing the bill at the restaurant. It's not that we can't learn new or different ways to think about our finances, but that change in mindset has to be intentional.

I grew up with a general sense of how money worked; you tithed, you saved, and you spent. Credit cards weren't really a thing my folks talked about, and debit cards didn't even exist back then. There were two things you didn't talk about at our supper table; who my parents voted for in the presidential election and how much money my dad made, so I had no idea about anything connected to budgeting. Our family of five went on vacations, had a lake house, drove used cars, and went out to eat every now and then. I knew we weren't rich but also that we didn't go without a lot. Honestly, I was never quite sure how any of the money "stuff" worked. I'm pretty sure I thought money just showed up when you needed it. I was clueless.

Kelly grew up in a household that didn't talk about money at all, and so he was also basically in the dark as to how to manage the household finances.

So, with both of us pretty much "winging it," we had a lot of hiccups in the early years. We overspent based on our income, we got into debt with credit cards, and when we got our first debit card, we forgot to write down our withdrawal receipts and overdrew our account multiple times. In our first few years of full-time ministry, we got some bad tax advice and owed thousands of dollars, most of which we paid with money we borrowed from my parents. It felt like we could never quite get ahead. I was the saver and Kelly was the spender, but I liked the spontaneous spending as well as he did, so my resolve to "not touch our savings" often didn't hold for very long.

We battled about money for years. I wanted to make sure we

always had a certain amount in savings, and Kelly wanted to make sure we were enjoying life. All the tension makes sense to me now; we weren't establishing our own way of thinking about money—we were just doing what we had observed. But back then, I thought it just might end our marriage. I thought he was irresponsible and he thought I was controlling and "parental."

We needed help, and the help we got had nothing to do with money. For what seemed forever, we just struggled on our own. We had friends that we got together with to play cards, eat pizza and watch movies, but that was all that sat on top of the "table" of our relationships. We hadn't yet established the kind of friendships where the things underneath the table, like money, sex, crisis of faith, etc., were talked about (thankfully, we have those friendships now). I was having a hard time with shame around this money issue, so, I was hesitant to talk to either set of our parents about it, because I felt like they would either try to fix it for us or judge us for it. We didn't even think about consulting our pastor at the time. Money didn't seem to be something you took to your spiritual leader, unless you were talking about tithing. So, for a long time we fumbled around in the darkness that money troubles can cause in a person's (or couple's) life.

It wasn't until we had been married about 15 years and we had completed a personality assessment called the DISC that we discovered the root of so many of the challenges we faced in our marriage. These difficult places in our relationship weren't confined to our approach to money. Rather what we were fighting against was actually about control. As in, who wanted to have all the power and be in control in our relationship. A very wise, older couple was walking us through the assessment results, and it was like a lightbulb went off. Remember when that Campus Pastor was very awkwardly trying to tell us to pay attention to something about the way we related to the world differently by asking us to postpone the wedding? Sitting at that couple's table, it hit me that this issue of power and control is what he was talking about. Because the answer to who wants to be in control in our relationship was both of us. Which, as I've gotten older and talked to more couples, seems pretty much like a human condition, not just a Kelly and Suze problem.

So, we walked away from that assessment debrief, got in our car and sat in that couple's driveway for what seemed like hours and decided that we were going to try to sort out this matter of power and control in our relationship. Like the unraveling of a really ugly sweater that neither of us liked but we kept wearing, we found out we weren't actually fighting about the $100 he spent on a pair of tennis shoes or how I wouldn't let us spend on a fancy meal out. We were arguing about who was going to make, what seemed to be, the "really important" decisions in our family. We affectionately labeled this kind of arguing as fighting about the "thing behind the thing." This discovery caused us to go on one of the most important fact finding journeys of our partnership so far: *do we trust God to provide for us more than we trust our own abilities to do so?*

> "Do we trust God to provide for us more than we trust our own abilities to do so?"

In the Bible, there's a story about God providing for his people as they are on their own journey of figuring out if they trust God more than they trust themselves. The book is entitled Exodus, because that's what the people of God, the Israelites, did—they "exited" Egypt and all they had been enslaved to there. They would end up living in the desert for 40 years with a whole generation dying before they emerged into the land God had promised them. In those four decades, God would provide for them in ways they never could have imagined or even known to ask for, and it began on the "fifteenth day of the second month after they left Egypt" (Exodus 16:1). They had run out of food and started complaining, wishing they had never started this adventure in the first place. God makes a promise to their leader, Moses, telling him that everyday bread will "rain down from heaven" and that the people should gather it in the morning, but they can only gather what they need for that day—no more, no less. If a family tried to keep more than they needed for the next day, the bread would be rotten. God was saying, "You can trust me to take care of the big things in your life, like getting you freed from slavery, as well as the small things, like food for the day."

And here's what I know: if God did it for His people then, He will do it for His people now. Maybe not in the form of bread lying on the ground each morning, but always more than plenty to see us through each day.

These days, money troubles are still a thing in our household, they just look different now. Our children are adults, and I worry we didn't give them all the tools they would need to navigate their own challenges with money. Instead of stepping into those situations and "fixing" them, we've chosen to answer questions when they ask, coach when we can, and pray like crazy. As I write this, Kelly and I are not making enough money to pay all our monthly bills. Kelly launched a business that got slammed by the pandemic, and I left a well-paying job to explore what God might have next for me. Both of these moves were steps of faith that may have looked stupid to some, but felt like obedience to us.

Don't be fooled by my confidence in that last sentence, in this season I'm finding this kind of obedience to be incredibly difficult. I LIKE it when there's enough money to take care of our responsibilities, and I feel "safe" (what does that even mean?) when I'm not worrying about finances. However, right now, while it doesn't make any sense "on paper," all our bills are getting paid. Because I'm still learning the lesson that God will always provide exactly what we need, when we need it; we just have to be willing to look for it and gather it while we can.

Jesus never wanted us to forget that miracle of the bread raining down from Heaven every morning. So, when his disciples asked them to teach them how to pray, one of the lines in that prayer says, "Give us this day, our daily bread" (Matthew 6:9-13). You take enough "daily bread" days and add them together, and you've lived a life that is evidence of the only kind of provision that matters.

TO CONSIDER

What lie have I believed about God's ability to provide?

What truth could replace this lie?

What will knowing this truth change about the way I'm living?

Because change isn't a solo undertaking, who, among my trusted friends can I tell about this discovery?

Exhibit D: Sometimes, You Don't Finish First

Loss, I've learned, is a deeply personal journey. Whether you've lost a job or a friendship or a treasured piece of jewelry, the road into, through, and out of that loss can sometimes feel like an odyssey. The only way to navigate it is to go through it. The only one that can get me through it is me, the one who is no longer holding the lost thing in my hand or heart.

I think it's important for everyone, at some point in their lives, to come face to face with the fact that sometimes, even if we have a plan that says the outcome will be otherwise, we don't come in first (or even finish at all). Still, there is always life afterwards. That life will be where the story gets told, and maybe (most likely) there might be some gratitude to be found for the losing.

Our kids were raised in the era of "everybody gets a trophy." My parents, 60 years their elders, thought this was stupid. When our son was in early elementary school, he played in a basketball league called "Hot Shots." It was organized and hosted by one of the local Christian schools in our town, and it seemed like a great opportunity to play some basketball, learn something about sportsmanship, and memorize some scripture. My parents came to a few Saturday morning games. and by a few, I mean two. The first game they attended, Ben's team was ahead by at least 20 going into halftime. When the kids came back out onto the court to start the second half, the scoreboard had changed, reflecting a tie ballgame. My Dad quickly pointed this out and with great fervor demanded to know who was responsible for this obvious error. Before he headed down to the scorekeepers bench, I informed Dad that in this league, the kids got points for memorizing scripture. So at halftime, in addition to the coach's pep talk, the kids were reciting passages of scripture, and if they did it correctly, they earned their team two points. My dad was flabbergasted. With big eyes and an even bigger voice declared, "What in the heck are you talking about? That is not how this game works. You get points by putting the ball through the hoop." After a little discussion, and much eye rolling on Dad's part, Grandpa calmed down and settled back into watching his Grandson play. For context, Dad was a member of the Indiana Basketball Hall of Fame. He played all through high school and college, then successfully coached in a state where basketball was king. In his experience, the winner was decided by skill and strategy on the court, not by short term memory skills. I'm pretty sure he was right.

There's been a lot written on the "everybody wins" philosophy and the ramifications it may or may not have had on an entire generation. That's a different discussion for a different time. What I do know is this: losing has been an important part of my character development. If I was under the illusion that I never have or never will lose, I believe it would be even more difficult than it already is to become a person of humility and honor. As well, I think it would be an even greater challenge than it is to sort out my true identity. If I had always made the team, never been told "no thanks" for that second interview, faithfully auditioned and yet never saw my name on the callback list, or never flunked a test, it's my theory that I would still be searching, as a woman in her late 50s, to figure out my core identity and purpose.

The greatest lesson not "winning" all the time has taught me is that the moment of failure, and it really is just a moment, passes quickly, and life will keep moving forward. When I have not been chosen to stand in the front of the line, I'm not left with no options. On the contrary, I can always decide to walk away or take a moment and figure out "what now?"

I've done both—and sometimes not very well.

One of the most difficult places to stand, for me at least, is on the outside looking in. Over the years of my life, I have desperately wanted to belong and to know that I mattered. So much so, that I have done some pretty dishonorable (not illegal or anything, just kind of "icky") things. Most of these actions were taken on with the sole purpose of making myself look better than I actually was. To hold my place in that winners line, if there ever was such a thing.

I had a tendency to overpromise and underdeliver for most of my growing up life, and probably would've kept at it, if it hadn't stopped working for me.

As you know now, I embellished stories, covered up my missteps, and downright lied to make sure no one saw my flaws. I would "Yes, I can absolutely get that done for you," knowing full well I had no idea HOW I was going to get it done. When I did NOT get "it" done, I would proceed to create a narrative around the not doing that made me either look like a victim or a hero. All of this worked, or so I thought, until a friend of mine cared about me enough to call me on it. She had observed me making promises and not keeping them. She had a kind of "sixth sense" for when I was lying about things. It was unsettling, but also incredibly transformative when she challenged me on things. When this trusted voice in my life lovingly said, "I don't believe you," or asked, "Is that what really happened?" It was like a scalpel between truth and fiction separating the unhealthy away from what was healthy in me. Like all surgeries, it was a painful and arduous process. It was a reckoning of sorts that happened quietly and privately without many people knowing.

But I knew, and what I knew was that I had made "covering up" an art form. Without that in place, I was exposed and vulnerable. Which was exactly where I needed to be. What if I wasn't the best or the brightest in the room? What if everyone saw through me and found out I wasn't actually that clever or creative? What if people began to see the real me—who would I be to them then? I was like an addict getting sober; no more half-truths or redirection when I thought I might look bad if someone found out.

For Lent one year, early in this process, I gave up lying. I felt like I was in that Jim Carey movie, where his son makes a wish that his Dad will only tell the truth except no one was laughing or paying me money to watch. The required path for me toward living a life of authenticity and vulnerability was through the practice of truth-telling—about myself primarily, but also about situations and people. I embarked on that journey because of an unbreakable promise: I belonged to God, no matter what.

Mind you, this wasn't a new truth. I had become a Christian when I was 12, but it was a truth I was finally going to trust enough to live. I am God's, even when I don't finish first. He called me daughter, even when I didn't feel like I was "enough" for my own parents. The name He chose for me was Beloved, and that is true even if no one else ever treated me that way again. The list could go on and on, because the adventure I went on as I laid down the deception and picked up Truth was life-changing. I began to see myself in ways that probably only God had up until that point.

As harsh as this may sound, I have a theory that everyone, at least once in their life, should be fired from a job, or get broken up with, or find themselves with an empty bank account. After I went into remission from my first Cancer, everyone treated me differently, like I might break at any moment, so I needed to be held gently and handled with kid gloves. I'm not gonna lie—I liked it. I was 15; what teenager in the world would say, "Hey everyone, could you stop giving me extra, quit letting me go first, no more treating me with kindness and giving me special treatment?"

"If you're not allowed to fail, or even if it very rarely occurs, you may not recognize it when it happens, and you sure as heck are not going to embrace it for the VERY NECESSARY character building process that it is."

My parents especially spent a lot of my time between the ages of 16 and 18 worried about me. They were plagued with the possibility of things like another diagnosis, a car accident, someone kidnapping me (one of the most common fears parents have about their kids), and other general worrisome possibilities. Their concern translated into me not being over-disciplined by them. I still had rules and boundaries, but I may or may not have pushed those limits a time or two. All of this permission, born out of their gratitude that I was still around, I understand now to be a big part of the origin of my needing to be "first." If you're not allowed to fail, or even if it very rarely occurs, you may not recognize it when it happens, and you sure as heck are not going to embrace it for the VERY NECESSARY character building process that it is.

I have had some pretty competitive people in my life over the years, and I have heard more than one of them say that coming in second is actually the first loser. My competitiveness comes out in trying to avoid anything that might not look like "first." For me, part of what I've learned in my journey into a more authentic way of living is that losing is necessary and, in my opinion, inevitable. Even someone with a beautifully laid out plan is going to lose, or at least not be first, at some point in their lives. They won't get the job, win the race, conceive the baby, make the marriage work, be chosen to be a part of the "inner circle", understand things other people seem to get, be liked by everyone, hold a popular opinion, or beat the Cancer.

And that is absolutely fine.

In fact, for me, it has become more than fine. It has been incredibly difficult, but still good because it is in the not winning every time, or at all, that I am invited to learn about leaning less on my own understanding (Proverbs 3:5-6) and leaning hard into God's goodness, faithfulness, provision, and love. This place of not being first has been where I've learned that I can fail and not be a failure, I can lose and not be a loser, and I can stand on the outside looking in and still belong.

TO CONSIDER

What lie have I believed about "winning," or at least being the best and the brightest, and what that says about my worth?

What truth could replace this lie?

What will knowing this truth change about the way I'm living?

Because change isn't a solo undertaking, who among my trusted friends can I tell about this discovery?

PART 8: THE END

LIE

There will be a time when you "arrive" (as in figure out your life and all its complexities) in life, and it's all smooth sailing from there.

TRUTH

Life is a journey packed full of joy and suffering, and the only "arriving" is at the end, when God decides it's time for the REAL adventure to begin.

When I first started thinking about writing a book that contained the stories of my life, I was fifteen years younger than I am now. I messed around with it, writing on and off, paying attention to it and then ignoring it for all that time. For years I thought I was supposed to write it, and others confirmed that my story was one they might want to read. Still, I didn't do it. Was it a lack of confidence that kept me from sitting down and doing it? Probably. Were there stories to tell that just hadn't happened yet? Maybe. Did I have thoughts and ideas that could only be said after my folks were gone? Possibly. Was I scared I wouldn't remember things or even have enough stories that anybody cared about reading? Absolutely.

For all those reasons and more, I didn't write—but then I did. When I began this book, my life had opened up and there was more "room." My dad had died, I was in between jobs, and I found someone to help guide me through the process. Earlier that year, someone who had no idea that I was contemplating writing my story posted this Anne Lamott quote on Facebook and tagged me in it:

> *"Oh my God, what if you wake up some day, and you're 65, or 75, and you never got your memoir or novel written, or you didn't go swimming in those warm pools and oceans all those years because your thighs were jiggly and you had a nice big comfortable tummy; or you were just so strung out on perfectionism and people-pleasing that you forgot to have a big juicy creative life, of imagination and radical silliness and staring off into space like when you were a kid? It's going to break your heart. Don't let this happen."*
>
> ANNE LAMOTT[1]

So, deep in my gut I knew it was time to write.

It was time to put down on paper (a screen actually) some truth about my journey so far.

It had taken me lots of years, and even more tears, to "rediscover Suze Fair"—to reconnect with my true self and find my voice. So it was probably the right time to use it.

As I have written (and rewritten) these stories, I've remembered a lot. I've thought about what it took to get me to believe some of the lies that were serving as a foundation for my life, and I've considered the work that has been required for me to break up with those lies and embrace greater, life-transforming truths. Mostly though, I've reflected on the goodness of God and how it shows in my life. More than once I've thought, "What a life I get to live," and I've said it with nothing but awe and gratitude.

My great grandma on my dad's side was a tiny, quiet woman whose name was Orella. She went by her middle name Delle, but we called her Grammy. She was gone before I got to build a relationship with her, but I knew her, and my memories of her are only of warmth, kindness, love, and K-Mart house dresses. When I arrived on the scene, she lived in a mobile home on the back of my grandparent's property. She was an independent, gentlewoman who had been married to a larger than life, loud, opinionated man the family called Pap. Oh the stories my dad told us about Pap—a man known for his work ethic and a propensity to cuss a little. Grammy and Pap were committed to their family, the community, and the local church. They raised three children in the Church of the Brethren. In this tradition, in those days, during the worship service the women and children sat on one side of the church while the men sat on the other. The women also wore prayer coverings (a little white cap made out of netting or cloth) on their heads as a sign of modesty and holiness. In the early 1920s, the denomination decided that this little piece of cloth was a mandatory accessory in order for a woman to enter the sanctuary. Based on the writing of the denomination and stories in my own family, this practice was comforting to some and demeaning to others. It was a practice that continued for years. My mom was also raised in the Church of the Brethren and wore a prayer covering until the early 1960s.

> "Belonging happens when we embrace the Truth that we are seen, known, and chosen by the One who imagined us into being, and nobody can take that away."

In 1905, my sweet, quiet Grammy decided she didn't need to wear a white piece of cloth on her head anymore to communicate anything about her faith or her love for God. My Grandmother, Grammy's daughter, gave me journals that documented lots of things about life for my great grandmother, and this switch in her approach to church life was just one. In one of the journal entries Grammy writes about getting a visit from the church Eldership, so they could have a "conversation" with her concerning her attempt to share in a church business meeting, without her husband's permission, and for not wearing her prayer covering. She was being disciplined for not following the rules—for not continuing to sit down and be quiet. As the journals give evidence, that first "conversation" would not be the last.

When I think about the women I most admire in the world, the list is pretty short and my great grandmother's name is at the top. Orella Delle Carper was a woman who supported her farmer husband, raised three children who would all go on to get not just their high school education, but university degrees and even Master's degrees. She survived horrible tragedies including a tornado that wiped out the family farm, and she remained committed to her faith and her family until the day she died. She found her voice in the church, in an age where that wasn't something women did, and she used it.

This story of my great grandmother makes me deeply proud and profoundly sad all at the same time. Proud because this woman is in me, she's in my sister, and she's in my daughters and nieces. All these women have a tenacity when it comes to fighting for what is right and wrong and that can be directly linked to Grammy's spunk. The story makes me sad, because it reminds me of how far we still have to go in the church, and in the world, when it comes to gender equality.

But mostly I'm proud, because Grammy knew who she was and that was whoever God said she was, not what was prescribed by the church Elders or a set of rules. She was whole and wonderful and brilliant because she was Orella Delle. Grammy wasn't brave enough to walk through those doors without her covering because she was a revolutionary; she did it because she knew what was a lie and what was the truth.

I think my great grandmother would have loved reading these stories of my life. I think she would have found glimpses of herself in them and been tickled by the similarities.

My prayer for what I've offered here is that these words will be like a signpost on a road you think you might be lost on, but it somehow seems familiar. Let these words be a reminder that life is a (hopefully) long adventure, filled with lots of "ups" and probably a few "downs." The goal is not mastering this life and the living of it, but rather to trust that every nook and cranny of the one life we've been given was done so by the Creator of the Universe.

Also, don't forget that belonging is not something that happens when you put on a prayer covering, get the job, marry the guy or gal, have the children, get healed from the disease, have enough money in the account, or fit into someone else's idea of who you should be or what you should do. Belonging happens when we embrace the Truth that we are seen, known, and chosen by the One who imagined us into being, and nobody can take that away.

End of story.

For now.

ACKNOWLEDGEMENTS

When it comes to gratitude, I feel full to overflowing. I want to take a minute and say "Thank you" to so many who have made this crazy 15 year journey of, "I think I'd like to write a book," to "It's time to write a book," possible.

First, to all of you who plopped down your resources so you could hold these words in your hands. What an honor it is to share these stories with you. I hope your own journey with confronting the lies that have been guiding you, so you can embrace the kind of truth that brings Joy, is as transformative as mine has been.

To every person who, over the years, has encouraged me to write. Whether it was subtle or overt, every one of those nudges led me here. Thank you.

To Joy Eggerichs Reed and Amelia Graves. There is absolutely NO WAY, on God's green earth, that this book would be here without your wisdom, guidance, and encouragement. The Writing Cohort was a game changer for me and I will always tell the story of those 30 days being the catalyst that got me unstuck and motivated on this book writing journey.

To Andy and Jordan Kurzen, thank you for investing your many gifts into this project. So much beauty—gah, that cover—and for that, my heart is so happy.

To every Doctor who completed all their schooling, passed their exams, and gathered up the experience they would need to be ready to be the head, hands, and heart that would help keep this fragile frame of mine running. Bless you.

To every man or woman who played a part in my transformation journey. Whether I paid you for it, or we were part of each other's spiritual journey - your words of wisdom and insightful questions pointed me toward change and growth. Stay curious.

To Mim and Jim, thank you. For the life that you created together that resulted in mine, for the love that we shared, and for teaching me about beauty, retirement planning, and laughter. I miss you both, deeply. Yet, even as I grieve, I'm mindful that your lives are now complete and whole and there's nothing else I could hope for you.

To my sister Dawn and brother Rob, I love you. For all the years of life that have been and for all those that will be, I am thankful. And for all those nieces and nephews (and now greats) that I'm crazy about, thanks!

To the offspring. Very few of these stories would mean anything without your lives as a part of mine. You have taught me things only children can offer a parent and for that, thank you doesn't cut it. Ben, for your faith, ideas for days, your optimism, and your laugh. Katie, for your encouragement, podcast partnership, wisdom way beyond your years, and your mad marketing skills. Mackenzie, for your truth telling, cheerleading when I got down, practical problem solving, and buckets of love.

There is no SuzeFair without KellyFair. Your love for me has held me close and spurred me on for all of these 38 years. Your belief in me has always been so much more than my own and I'm confident I would have quit (so many things) long ago, if it hadn't been for your loving and honest partnership. Thank you for every "ledge" you've talked me down from and for all the moments, big and small, when your steadfast commitment to us and our calling has been the kick in the butt I needed. You are IT for me. Forever and always, Amen.

SOURCES

Introduction

1. Oliver, Mary, *New and Selected Poems*. Beacon Press, 1992.

Part 1: The Body

1. *The Message: The Bible in Contemporary Language*. Edited by Eugene H. Peterson, Nav Press, 2005.

2. McBride, Hillary, *The Wisdom of Your Body: Finding Healing, Wholeness, and Connection through Embodied Living*. Brazos Press, 2021.

Part 2: Faith

1. Lewis, C.S., *Voyage of the Dawn Treader*. Macmillan Company, 1965.

Part 3: Relationships

1. Berry, Wendell, *Hannah Coulter*. Counterpoint Publishing, 2005.

2. Weissbourd, Batanova, Lovison, and Torres (2021). *Loneliness in America: How the Pandemic Has Deepened an Epidemic of Loneliness and What We Can Do About It*. Retrieved from https://www.makingcaringcommon.org

3. Gary Thomas, *Sacred Marriage: What If God Designed Marriage to Make Us Holy More Than to Make Us Happy?* Zondervan, 2015.

4. & 5. Anonymous, *Prayer of St. Francis*

Part 4: Work

1. Manning, Brennan, *Ruthless Trust: The Ragamuffin's Path to God*, HarperCollins, 2009.

2. Buechner, Frederick, *Wishful Thinking: A Seeker's ABC*, Mowbry, 1994.

3. Palmer, Parker J., *The Courage to Teach : Exploring the Inner Landscape of a Teacher's Life*. Jossey-Bass, 1998.

Part 5: Emotions

1. Brown, Brené, *Daring Greatly: How the Courage to be Vulnerable Transforms the Way We Live, Love, Parent, and Lead*. Avery, 2012

2. & 3. Cowen and Keltner, *Self-report captures 27 distinct categories of emotion bridged by continuous gradients*, Berkeley News, 1994.

4. The National Centre Against Bullying, *Bullying Defined*. Retrieved from https://www.ncab.org.au/bullying-advice/bullying-for-parents/definition-of-bullying/

5. Chestnut, Beatrice PhD, *The Complete Enneagram: 27 Paths to Greater Self-Knowledge*. She Writes Press, 2013.

Part 6: True Self

1. Thomas Merton, *New Seeds of Contemplation*. New York: New Directions Books, 1972.

2. Benner, David, *The Gift of Being Yourself: The Sacred Call to Self-Discovery*. IVP Books, 2015.

3. Borland, James (2017). *How Jesus Viewed and Valued Women*. Retrieved from https://www.crossway.org/articles/how-jesus-viewed-and-valued-women/

4. Imes and Clance, *The Imposter Phenomenon in High Achieving Women: Dynamics and Therapeutic Intervention*. Retrieved from https://mpowir.org/wp-content/uploads/2010/02/Download-IP-in-High-Achieving-Women.pdf

5. Rohr, Richard (2015). *True Self, False Self*. Retrieved from https://cac.org/wp-content/uploads/2015/11/7-TRUE-SELF-FALSE-SELF.pdf

Part 7: The Plan

1. Rohr, Richard, *Breathing Underwater*. Franciscan Media, 2021.

Part 8: The End

1. Lamott, Anne (2014). Retrieved from author's Facebook page: https://www.facebook.com/AnneLamott

229

Made in the USA
Monee, IL
23 November 2022

18346866R20131